TRABERT ON TENNIS

The View From Center Court

TONY TRABERT
WITH GERALD SECOR COUZENS

CONTEMPORARY
BOOKS
CHICAGO · NEW YORK

Library of Congress Cataloging-in-Publication Data

Trabert, Tony.
    Trabert on tennis : the view from center court / Tony Trabert with
Gerald Secor Couzens.
        p.   cm.
    ISBN 0-8092-4664-3 : $17.95
    1. Tennis—United States.   I. Couzens, Gerald Secor.   II. Title.
GV1001.2.U6T73   1988
796.32'3'0973—dc19   88-1835
                                             CIP

Published by Contemporary Books, Inc.
180 North Michigan Avenue, Chicago, Illinois 60601
Manufactured in the United States of America
Library of Congress Catalog Card Number: 88-1835
International Standard Book Number: 0-8092-4664-3

Published simultaneously in Canada by Beaverbooks, Ltd.
195 Allstate Parkway, Valleywood Business Park
Markham, Ontario L3R 4T8 Canada

To my wife Vicki
and our lovely children.
—T.T.

To my wife Elisa
and our sprouting athletes.
—G.S.C.

Contents

Foreword

I first saw Tony Trabert around 1942, when I was playing in the Tri-State Tennis Championships held at the Cincinnati Tennis Club.

As I was departing the club one day after finishing my matches, I noticed a chubby 12-year-old in shorts, T-shirt, and visor practicing his volley. He was over-swinging at the shot. I asked someone who he was. That person told me he was Tony Trabert. I asked whether Tony was likely to mind my making an observation. Assured that he wouldn't, I strolled onto the court and introduced myself. I pointed out that he could improve the shot by punching it rather than swinging at it. He caught on in about 60 seconds, and, needless to say, I was impressed.

It was the beginning of a long and valued friendship.

Since that time, Tony has been a world-class player, captain of the U.S. Davis Cup team, a teacher, and a TV commentator. In all his years as a vital part of tennis,

Tony has amassed an incredible knowledge of the game—the politics, the personalities (of players and officials), and just what makes everything tick.

Trabert on Tennis is a book that will fascinate all tennis devotees. Tony has an insight that enables him to discuss intelligently the juniors, the high-powered pros, the tennis establishment (with the unending bickerings between the principals), the vast sums of money in the game, and the demise of the United States as a power in men's tennis. In short, *Trabert on Tennis* taught me a great deal about a game I've been connected with for almost 60 years.

To coin a phrase, the book is—in every sense of the word—a "well-punched volley!"

—Bill Talbert
Member, International Tennis
Hall of Fame

Foreword

Every once in a while, I come across a sports book that grabs my attention. Tony Trabert's book is one of these rare few. His observations on the current state of tennis are insightful. You won't be disappointed with his frank, in-depth appraisal.

One day in 1948 when I was playing Bobby Riggs for the pro title, we were playing in a high school gym in Cincinnati. Tony Trabert and his dad came by the locker room after the matches and we had a short visit. Bill Talbert had been telling everybody that a real talent was coming out of Cincinnati, and boy, was Bill right!

Tony won the national Junior Indoors singles and doubles in 1948 and he was on his way. Because Tony was climbing the ladder of amateur tennis and I was trying to stay on top of the pro game, we only made contact occasionally. I watched him play enough to know that his shots were very sound and that he got the most out of his game. He was a competitor and could handle pressure. If he had a problem, it might have been his mobility; he always had to beat that old demon, weight (had he chosen to play football or any other sport he probably would have weighed in at 210 to 215 pounds). As a tennis player, to play his best, he had to weigh under 185. It tells you something about Tony when I say he always made his playing weight. Tony had the dedication, skills, and drive of a champion.

Of course, another reason I always had great interest in how Tony was doing on the circuit was that he was using my Wilson Jack Kramer Autograph racket. He helped make it a household name from 1949 throughout 1956 when Wilson started making a Trabert racket.

I had a chance to get to know Trabe well in 1951 when the Davis Cup captain, Frank Shields, asked me to accompany the team to Australia. We had a talented squad—veteran Ted Schroeder, Wimbledon champion Dick Savitt, future U.S. and Wimbledon champion Vic Seixas, and the talented youngsters Tony Trabert and Hamilton Richardson. At this point I had seen enough of Tony, both on and off the court, to know that he was something special. I knew that he would be a great force in tennis for a long time. He was great to work with, very open to any suggestion that might improve his game, and always put out maximum effort in practice.

Trabe improved his game on this Australian tour but finally won the big one, Forest Hills, in 1953, and Wimbledon in 1955. Since I had defended my pro title against Frank Sedgman, I started thinking that maybe Tony and I might hook up on one of those grinding 100-match pro tours. But by the time Tony turned pro, I wasn't on the other side of the net anymore.

Not long after, Tony took over the management of my

European pro tennis operation. It meant moving to Paris, working full-time to schedule matches and tournaments, and basically trying to bring the two games of tennis—amateur and pro—together. We had quite a number of players under contract and we had to keep them busy; Tony did a great job making the European operation stronger and profitable. We formed a player association in 1962, and Tony was chosen to be its first executive director. His main goal was to bring about open tennis. We were ahead of our time; it was another six years before it came to be.

It was in 1972, a year after he had started his tennis camp, that CBS brought Tony into the TV box. I was on the CBS team, too, and knew immediately that Tony was going to be a great analyst. Tony's been there ever since, and has made all of the U.S. Opens and many other tennis telecasts very enjoyable for all sports fans. In 1976 the USTA asked Tony to captain the Davis Cup team, a position he held for five years. His teams won the Cup in 1978 and 1979—another great effort!

Tony Trabert has been involved in all phases of tennis; now he makes another contribution to the game in the form of this excellent book of insight, information, and advice. No one is more qualified.

Over the years, Tony has played a lot of tennis. His recognition as an authority stems from his accomplishments as a player who successfully fought all the major tennis battles around the world. His knowledge of the intricacies of the game was further developed by coaching and managing. Tony's career as a broadcast journalist, however, has afforded him a unique opportunity to observe the game from a different angle, a fact that is quite apparent in this compelling look at the game he loves so much.

Professional tennis, the youngest of all the major professional sports, is a game still trying to set a proper course for itself. Tony's astute analysis of the current state of tennis, focusing on the dearth of top American players, the influence of agents on the players and the game's structure, and the impact of exhibition matches on regularly scheduled tournaments is right on target. Equally vivid and throught-provoking is his behind-the-scenes look at what it takes for a young player to reach the big time.

Tony's revelations about the realities of the pro game may surprise some tennis fans, shock some others. But his well thought-out solutions, if followed, can certainly help alleviate many of the problems that now beset the game.

I tip my hat to Tony, and am delighted that he asked me to do a foreword to this book—I think it's terrific!

—Jack Kramer
Member, International Tennis
Hall of Fame

Acknowledgments

We wish to thank Marshall Happer III, administrator, and William L. Babcock, assistant administrator, of the Men's Tennis Council. Both men were extremely helpful in offering their insights into the pro game.

We also wish to thank our tireless editor, Stacy Prince. Her suggestions and thoughtful editing of the manuscript is much appreciated.

And thanks of course to Jim Trupin, literary agent, tennis maven, sports aficionado. He had an idea one autumn night about pro tennis.

Introduction

Professional tennis is in trouble. The business of tennis may be booming, but tennis as a professional sport is still suffering from growing pains. Only 20 years have passed since the advent of open tennis, when pros were finally allowed to compete with amateurs in the same events, and this makes tennis the youngest of all the major pro sports. As the game now tries to push into a more mature era with some sense of identity and a clear picture of where it's heading, it is encountering problems from some players, from powerful sports agents, and from just trying to shed its ties with its amateur roots.

Something is lacking in the pro tennis that I watch today. An essential element seems to have been lost between the time players first received payment for winning tournaments back in 1968 and today, when pro players are involved in what almost amounts to a global money chase.

1

I'm upset with the demeanor of some of today's tennis professionals. I'm annoyed with professional tennis players as a group of athletes. Too many of them are spoiled, self-centered, and unwilling to help nurture the game that has given so much to them.

Without a doubt, tennis suffered an inevitable loss of innocence when it went big time in 1968. We saw one extreme 30 years ago, when players had to struggle to find ways to cover basic living expenses in order to survive. Today we have the opposite extreme, where many players seem more concerned about choosing the best money manager than about turning in a quality performance. There seems to be no middle ground anymore for an athlete who wants to play a game that was once considered a "gentlemen's sport."

Men's professional tennis is big business. The players—more than 1,500 independent contractors hailing from more than 100 countries—owe allegiance to no one. Each one fights desperately for one of the several hundred spots in the world ranking, and the players' obligations are seemingly only to themselves and the achievement of personal success.

It was much different when I played the game. I looked at myself as a highly trained athlete who used my skills in a contest where my major responsibility was to offer the best tennis every time I played. I owed this to the spectators, my opponent, and myself. Today, far too many players seem to be entertainers with an overbooked schedule of one-nighters. The result is that, in this relentless pursuit of money, the sport I once knew has been lost, replaced by something that sports marketers have simply termed "product."

I have no regrets about my own tennis career. The sport gave me a wonderful opportunity to enjoy and accomplish more than I had ever dreamed possible.

Since I retired from the game as an active player in 1963, I've kept current with the sport as a television analyst who's often on the road more than 150 days out of the year. Over the years, I have marveled at how prize monies have escalated and how the tennis organizations have struggled to make themselves ever more professional.

These are certainly critical times for professional tennis. Thanks to a $35 million world tour and no strong, centralized form of administrative power such as exists in other pro sports, a power struggle has developed. The different factions within tennis—the players, agents, and the Men's Tennis Council (MTC)—are vying to take the game in a different direction. This is already causing serious problems.

I have strong opinions about what's wrong and also what's right with the game I care about so much. The following chapters give detailed explanations about the present state of pro tennis, describing what's going on behind the scenes and in the courts, where some skirmishes between the MTC and agents have already taken place. But although I'm annoyed by many of the flaws of the game, I'm still optimistic that positive changes can be made.

Tennis needs to be improved on both the professional and recreational level as it pushes into the 21st century. If the game is to arrive in the next century with a strong and interested following, then the game's national and international administrators will have to solve the problems now facing the sport. My suggestions, I hope, will help.

1
The Wunderkinder

Professional tennis has increasingly been dominated by precocious kids who pack a wallop with their rackets. They jump from age-group match-ups one week to Centre Court at Wimbledon the next. Two West German stars not yet out of their teens have already made their mark on the tennis world. Boris Becker won his first Wimbledon title in 1985, defeating Kevin Curren 6–3, 6–7, 7–6, 6–4 in a thrilling final. Just 17 years old at the time, Becker was actually several months younger than the eventual winner of the Junior Wimbledon title.

Another wunderkind, Steffi Graf, broke into the women's Top 10 at 16, eventually bumping Martina Navratilova and Chris Evert from the highest perch in 1987. By that time, she was a ripe old 18. Graf's presence at the top marked only the first time in 12 years that someone other than Navratilova, Evert, or giant killer Tracy Austin ruled the women.

In front of the pack of talented whiz kids was Californian Tracy Austin, now retired prematurely from the game because of a recurring back ailment. Austin had two U.S. Open titles to her name by the time she was 18 and was ranked Number 1 in the world for all of two months. Pam Shriver, now 25, was the youngest finalist in the U.S. Open when she was still a Maryland high school sophomore in 1978. John McEnroe, the scourge of the tennis world at one time, left Stanford University in 1978 after only one year. At 19 he seemed to move effortlessly right into the world of big-time tennis. Mats Wilander helped the world forget countryman Bjorn Borg when he won the French Open in 1981 at the age of 17. He is yet another of the Top 10 players that Sweden seems to be cranking off the assembly line like Volvos.

The youthful tennis successes of Evert, Becker, McEnroe, Graf, Austin, Shriver, Andrea Jaeger, and a host of other teenagers, remarkable though they may be, have set a bad precedent. Too many parents hold these talented teens up as examples for their kids. Their rationale seems to be, "If Boris can do it, so can you, Johnny." Unfortunately for the American player, it doesn't always work out the way the parents want.

The lure of lucre and the attraction of an all-expenses-paid college education have driven many American parents to extremes with their tennis-playing progeny. The results haven't always been laudable.

Proportionately, when compared to other countries, we do not have a lot of kids playing tennis in the United States, and some critics believe that the few who are playing are under an inordinate amount of pressure from parents, coaches, and themselves to win at an early age. Winning gives these kids prestige and a sense of identity, but winning can also cause problems.

Throughout its history, tennis has had a handful of precocious teen stars within its ranks. Talented players such as West Germany's Steffi Graf, who broke into the top ten at the tender age of 16 and became No. 1 at 18, and countryman Boris Becker, who won Wimbledon when he was 17, are the exception rather than the norm in a sport where victory usually goes to older, more experienced players.

Unlike other sports, tennis awards more than just ribbons and trophies to talented youngsters. If little Johnny or Mary proves to be a good tennis player during puberty, this entitles the child to hundreds of dollars worth of free equipment from manufacturers. Little kids fight hard to preserve this grub stake, and they subsequently begin to take fewer and fewer risks on the court, sticking to a style of play that will best assure them instant gratification—and more free equipment.

Consistent winning at a young age can also breed more serious psychological problems when the players get older and are regularly confronted with stiffer competition from more talented players. Sports psychologists are now reporting that once these precocious kids push on into their teens and start losing, far too few know how to accept their defeat. Instead, they often confuse their on-court loss with a loss of personal self-worth.

When it comes to having youngsters play tennis, the biggest problem lies not with the kids, but with the hordes of parents who goad them to succeed, who tag along, often abusing their children and anyone else within earshot when things don't go their way on the court.

Many years ago in Los Angeles, I regularly instructed Kathy May, a high school girl with a lot of promise who eventually was ranked seventh in America and twelfth in the world. Kathy often practiced with a friend—let's call her Mary—and Kathy would regularly beat her 6-1, 6-2. After their matches, Mary often would ask Kathy whether it was all right to tell her father that she had lost 7-5, 6-4 instead. Kathy, who sympathized with her friend's plight, agreed to go along with the ruse and never said anything to Mary's father.

Once I had the misfortune of sitting with him in the

stands during a match in which Kathy was playing. Toward the end of the first set, he watched in astonishment as Kathy went up to the umpire and pointed out that her previous shot had actually gone through the net and not over it, so the point should go to her opponent. The umpire thanked her and gave the point to the other girl.

"I'd never want Mary to admit something like that," he told me. "She's not out there to win the damn sportsmanship award. She's out there to win. Period."

"With you coaching her, I don't think your daughter will have to worry about winning any sportsmanship award," I tossed back at him. Somehow, the message didn't seem to sink in.

A couple of years after this incident, I went to San Francisco with Kathy for her first attempt at qualifying to become a professional and join the Virginia Slims tour. To prevent any possible problems during a quarterfinal match between Kathy and Mary, I talked to the referee and requested a full complement of linespeople, and he agreed.

"Whoever wins today is going to win with a tennis racket and intelligence, and not through cheating," I told him.

Kathy went on to crush Mary quite handily 6–0, 6–1, and there were no outbursts or calls to the linespeople from Mary or her father. But the defeat proved tough for both of them, as I would soon find out. Five minutes after the match, Kathy was calling her dad with the good news. As I stood outside the phone booth, I looked down the hallway and saw Mary and her sister, another aspiring player, crying into their hands.

Their father was castigating them for being losers and was pacing back and forth, ranting and raving at the two of them. He didn't stop this verbal assault until

the girls, along with their distraught mother, walked
away from him and his harangue, which started echo-
ing off cold concrete walls.

Stories like this rarely have happy endings. Needless
to say, neither Mary nor her sister plays competitive tennis on the circuit anymore. I don't blame them. If I had
had such a tyrant for a father, I'm sure that he would
have killed all the enjoyment in the sport for me. After
some time, I probably would have moved on to a sport
that didn't entail his involvement and might have pre-
served our relationship.

Since tennis isn't a team sport, parents often have to
play a much larger role than they do in any other sport.
Go to any junior tennis match, whether it's in Kalamazoo, Michigan, for the National 16s or 18s Championships; Miami for the annual Easter Bowl tournament; or
even a local club tournament in your own hometown.
You don't have to look very hard to find the "tennis
parents." They're the ones who haul around their own
aluminum lawn chairs and coolers so they can sit
courtside to proffer encouragement and coaching tips,
bite their nails, or simply bask in the enjoyment of their
children's play.

Not all tennis parents fit the overbearing stereotype,
but quite a few manage to transgress the standards of
acceptable behavior. One incident that shocked many
bystanders occurred during the 1987 Easter Bowl in
Miami, a prestigious tournament that attracted 380 juniors from around the country and at least 200 of their
parents. One oafish father was so disturbed by his
daughter's subpar play that he publicly berated her
courtside. Then, so as not to show any nepotism, he
verbally abused her opponent as well. When his daughter eventually lost her match (how did she stand a
chance not to?), the enraged man took his portable

cooler and hurled it out across a parking lot, screaming at the top of his lungs. What a fine example for our young people!

A lot of pressures come with being a top-rated junior tennis player. Trying to succeed at this level often affects not only the player and his or her parents, but brothers and sisters as well. It can have a devastating impact on family life.

For many parents, the financial burdens of junior tennis are enormous, and some don't let their children forget it. According to a survey of parents at the Easter Bowl conducted by Seena Hamilton, the founder and organizer of that tournament, it costs an average of $5,000 to $10,000 a year to keep Junior on the courts with clothing, equipment, and lessons. In addition, long practice hours, private lessons, stays at tennis academies, and travel far and wide to play in tournaments are required to build a national ranking in 12–under, 14–under, 16–under, and 18–under categories. All of this can easily translate to lost summer vacations, a reordering of family priorities, and strained sibling relations. More importantly, valuable time is stolen away from sharing some of the most simple basic family experiences—time that can never be recovered.

Of the thousands who play in junior tennis, only a rare few are able to cut back on expenses by being selected to be on the Junior Davis Cup squad and Junior Wightman Cup team, two elite team groups that pay all expenses for the players. Most others, unfortunately, learn about economic sacrifices at an early age. More often than not, they are reminded of it regularly.

As a result, many pressures on the junior players are self-imposed. They think that they have to succeed in order to please their parents, who have not only invested their interest and time in their training, but a good deal of money as well. Kids know they have to succeed in order to keep their name on the manufacturers' lists for free tennis equipment. Above all, they feel they must win in order to earn a college athletic scholarship.

A good way to avoid all of these problems is for the parents to sit down regularly with their son or daughter and to discuss their child's aspirations, expectations, and future plans. Tennis is a great sport physically and mentally. Preventing it from becoming the complete focus of a family's activities allows a youngster to experience the joys that come with being a teenager without the unnecessary emotional burdens of trying to achieve unrealistic tennis goals.

Although many kids dream of a pro life, very few juniors will actually go on to become successful professionals. It will therefore be very interesting to follow the fledgling pro career of Michael Chang, a high school sophomore from Plancentia, California. Chang, 15, was one the best juniors in the world and had been favorably compared to Boris Becker and John McEnroe at the same age. In 1987 Chang won the Boys National 18s Championship at Kalamazoo, Michigan, thereby earning a wild-card entry to the U.S. Open. He was only the fifth player under the age of 16 to play in the men's championships since the tournament was open to pros and amateurs in 1968. (But as young as Chang was—15 years, 6 months, and 30 days old—even younger players have participated in the Open. In 1979, Kathy Horvath turned 14 just five days before the tournament began.)

Although the odds were against Chang's going past the first round, he defeated 32-year-old Australian Paul McNamee to become the youngest male ever to win a match at the U.S. Open. In the second round, he pushed Nigerian Nduka Odizor to five sets before finally falling 6–1, 6–7 (9–7), 3–6, 6–4. Because of his success at the

Open and at subsequent Grand Prix events, Chang's ATP ranking shot from 970 in the world to 163.

In January 1988, Chang opted to turn pro after receiving a long-term contract to endorse Reebok athletic shoes and clothing. Chang, whose parents have spent more than $100,000 for lessons, travel, and equipment, told *World Tennis* magazine that he was turning pro because he felt an obligation to assist his parents financially.

Still, I think Michael Chang and his parents are taking a big gamble. By going on the pro tour at this young age, Chang stands a good chance of being ground down both mentally and physically by the tour veterans who will catch on very quickly to his baseline game. I liken what he's attempting to do to talented young boxers who are rushed along in order to attempt to capitalize on their potential. Unfortunately, what usually happens is just the opposite. When you push too fast, you may get some preliminary results that look encouraging. You may even win a good sum of money. But when the time finally comes when you should be in your prime, there may not be any spark or enthusiasm left for the game. The end result is that one's true potential is never realized.

A great many juniors go on to win college scholarships, thereby advancing their education as well as getting coaching and competition for four years. Most, like Kathy May, will continue to play tennis for fun and enjoyment once their tournament playing days are over. The fun that comes from playing the game to the best of one's ability—not the incessant striving for victory—is the essence of this sport. If parents would only realize this early on in the athletic careers of their children, everyone—especially the junior players—would be better for it.

2
The Early Games

While an overflow crowd and I watched Michael Chang play at Court 16 at the 1987 U.S. Open, I couldn't help thinking back to my own up-bringing and how I started playing tennis on the playground courts of Cincinnati so many years ago. No highly sophisticated developmental system for junior players was in place when I was learning how to play. There were local and state tournaments, as well as the national tournaments, but we didn't have any special camps, clinics, academies, or developmental programs. Along the way, we honed our skills and studied our opponents' games to pick up any worthwhile tips. As a player got better, he or she rose to the top by knocking off everyone who came along. Those who lost either tried again or else gradually drifted away from the game.

My dad, Arch, loved all sports and was a big inspiration in my life. He was a strong man physically, but stronger still was his sense of ethics, honesty, and fair play. Before entering the University of Nevada, where he earned five letters, including one for tennis, he used to box in amateur fights all over the West. He had always encouraged me in sports generally. When it came to tennis, which happened to be his favorite, he was there to offer pointers or to hit with me whenever I needed a partner. He never needed to use much prompting to get me to play the game. "Tennis, anyone?" he'd ask, and I was usually the first to get my racket.

Growing up in Cincinnati with two older brothers, Marc and Doug, I got to play a lot of tennis, as well as a lot of baseball and basketball in their seasons. My dad firmly believed that if we were occupied with sports most of the time, we'd stay out of trouble. Since I enjoyed sports so much, I had no difficulty following his advice. It worked, too!

One unforgettable piece of advice he gave me came when I was seven years old. I was playing tennis on the courts at the playground just down from our house and not really doing all that well. It was early evening, and my returns were flying everywhere but in bounds. Finally, frustrated by the whole process, I heaved my racket over the high chain link fence and stormed around acting mad at the world. At this point, my senses told me that someone was staring at me, and I turned to see my father behind the fence at the other end of the court. He stuck his index finger through the fence and silently motioned me to come over to him.

I remember this vividly because, at the time, it felt like the longest walk I ever took. When I finally got to the fence, he bent down and said to me, "If you ever do something like that again, I'll drop you like a hot potato." Then he turned and walked back home.

That ended my racket-throwing days for good. In light of what I've seen on courts in this country and abroad, many parents must have wished they'd done the same thing with their children at an early age.

Although I've competed around the world and played in hundreds of tennis tournaments, one tournament that I'll never forget is, like the oft-mentioned first kiss, my very first one. The year was 1940, and I was all of 10 years old. I had received special permission from my principal to be released from school a few hours earlier than usual this warm spring day. I thought I was a big shot leaving my classmates behind while I went off with my racket, white shorts, and T-shirt. I was full of confidence and bluster (as well as a little fear) as I ambled over to the 15-and-under boys' tournament in the park. My first-round opponent that day was a big kid named Don White, a 15-year-old who also happened to be the number 1 seed.

My dad sat on the bench with Don's father, and in no time he beat me 6–0 in the first set. I was certainly overmatched, but I continued to struggle on. With the few skills that I had, I quickly fell behind 3–0 in the second set and was fading fast. It looked like it was going to be 6–0, 6–0, but I still tried to do all I could to get some points for myself. I might not have been all that good, but at least I was determined.

When we changed sides to begin the fourth game of the 2nd set, Don suddenly walked over to the fence and began talking to his father. I took this moment to give myself a pep talk and also to try to get my nerves calmed down.

Miraculously, my serve picked up right after this short break, and I was able to win the next game from White. My father gave me the thumbs-up sign and had a big smile on his face. For me, this softened the blow of losing all those other games and gave me the encouragement that I needed to go on.

I eventually lost 6–1 and was knocked out of the tour-

When I started playing tennis as a youngster, equipment was very basic: white shorts, a T-shirt, wooden racket, sneakers, and plenty of determination. Unlike today, there weren't any tennis camps, clinics, academies, or special developmental programs. **PHOTO COURTESY OF THE TRABERT ARCHIVES**

nament, but I didn't feel too bad as I went home with my dad. "I was able to get at least one game off a big teenager," I remember saying.

My father smiled down at me, patted me on my head, and told me that there would be better days in time as long as I continued to practice hard and never give up.

About three years later, my dad finally admitted that he, Don, and Don's father had agreed during that impromptu timeout to let me "win" at least one game in the tournament so I wouldn't feel so bad.

By the time I was 13 years old, I was a die-hard Cincinnati Reds fan, and I had also become a better baseball catcher than tennis player. One warm summer night, my father sat me down after he got home from work and told me that I should consider making an important decision.

"Choose the sport that you want to spend the most time with," he said in that quiet, unhurried manner of his. "You've got the ability to be good in both sports, but if you don't give one your complete attention, then you'll never get to reach the full potential that I think you have. You'll just be average like 99 percent of the people in the world. I think you can be special."

Up until that time, I had always been a team player and liked playing basketball and baseball with my friends. But I also liked the idea of being out there on my own in tennis. When I did something well, I could take credit for it. And if I blew a shot or double faulted, I'd have to take the rap. Without hesitation, I told my dad that I would quit baseball. Ever since that night, I haven't looked back.

In the early 1940s when I started playing, tennis was simpler in a lot of ways. But walking around in those little white shorts, I got funny looks from people. It seemed that you weren't a real athlete in Cincinnati unless you were in a sport where you were knocking someone down. Tennis players were considered the "pansies" of the athletic world, a limp-wristed group of guys who weren't talented enough to make the team in any other sport.

I managed to ignore all the stares, taunts, and comments because I was in love with tennis and the challenge that the game offered. I liked hitting the darn ball where I wanted it, counteracting what my opponent was trying to do to me. My motivation to play came strictly from within. The idea of trying to win and become the best player that I could was enough reason to keep heading back to the courts day after day, full of enthusiasm and determination.

Although tennis was certainly popular then, and most matches were covered by the press, it was much more low-key than it is today. My high school tennis coach wasn't a $20-a-half-hour teaching pro, but a man who happened to be the school custodian. Our tennis team would spend a lot of time hitting balls against a big cement wall at the school, using the public courts five miles away for organized practices and matches. Still, playing under conditions that would seem woefully inadequate to most parents of today's budding junior stars, I managed to win the Ohio State high school tennis singles title three years in a row.

By my senior year, I was offered college scholarships from several West Coast universities known for their hotshot tennis teams, but instead I chose to stay at home and go the University of Cincinnati. The university had no indoor tennis facilities, so in the winter I played on the basketball team to keep in shape. To keep from losing too much contact with tennis, I would go down to my old high school, Walnut Hills, with a few of my tennis buddies, and we'd chalk in some lines on the polished basketball court and play a few sets on the weekends. Talk about fast court conditions!

The University of Cincinnati was hardly one of the high-pressure tennis factories that are now so common in the United States. Coached by a local pro, George Menefee, who later worked as trainer for the Los Angeles Rams football team, I went undefeated in singles, eventually winning the 1951 NCAA Singles Championships.

While I was at Cincinnati, I made a lot of friends through tennis and also from playing on the basketball team. During spring break one year, the tennis team went south to get in some matches and practice in the warm weather. Traveling down with us was a friend of mine who came to Cincinnati from New York on a basketball scholarship. We got to talking on this trip about sports and how we thought we could do in sports other than the ones we played most of the time.

It was then that I suggested to Sandy Koufax that he go out for the baseball team, something he had been thinking about but hadn't done. He later took me up on my suggestion, and although he initially had a difficult time getting the ball over the plate, he later went on to do quite well for himself pitching for the Brooklyn and Los Angeles Dodgers for 12 seasons. He retired from the game at 30 with an arthritic elbow and six years later was inducted into the Baseball Hall of Fame, the youngest ever to receive the honor.

One of the greatest benefits of staying in Cincinnati was having my dad there to give me help and encouragement. He was my biggest fan and supporter and came to watch many of my practice sessions at the university after he finished work at General Electric Company.

By his own admission, my dad wasn't that good a tennis player. He used to say that what fine points he learned about the game came from asking the pros to explain how or why they did something on the court, and by reading tennis books and studying matches. He'd go through it all with me step by step until he was sure I understood. My dad was always constructively critical of my game, yet understanding, something that many parents today are not. For that reason alone, I never resented his help. Instead, I welcomed it.

Even though tennis was erroneously thought of as a country club sport, in which all the top players had been born with silver spoons in their mouths, none of the friends I played tennis with came from rich families. When I first started playing, there was never any money to be made in tennis, so it was the love of the sport and the competition that drove us to keep playing. The public's attitude was just a throwback to the aristocratic origins of tennis in England in the mid-19th century.

Tennis was originally embraced by the rich, a sport played only by ladies and gentlemen on the wide, neatly clipped lawns of sprawling English country estates, or else at private membership clubs that sprang up with tennis as their focal activity. Croquet and badminton— two forms of athletic endeavor popular among the rich before Major Walter Clopton Wingfield invented tennis in 1873—quickly gave way to donning the white outfits favored by cricket players and having a go at this new game. Not only did the nobility of England begin to take a liking to the game, but it became popular with the military, which did its best to export tennis to all British outposts that had a spot of available grass on which to mark a tennis court. When the game came to the United States, it was set up in private clubs and on huge estates, where it was played by people with money. It was these tennis clubs that spawned and supported what was to become the tennis circuit in this country.

In the summer months, whenever young players traveled to play in amateur tournaments out of town, few had the money to spend for hotels, so it was common for the host club to make arrangements with club members to put up the visiting players. In the late 1940s I recall traveling to Massachusetts to play in the National Doubles Championships, which were being held at the Longwood Cricket Club. Due to a delay along the way from Cincinnati, I arrived at the club late Sunday night, the day before the tournament was to begin, and to my dismay the club was all locked up. Not knowing where to go and since I had set aside just enough money to cover my meals, I had no other recourse than to sleep out on the lawn of the club. The next day I was awakened by some startled club officials, who apologized for my having had to sleep under the stars and then took me to the home I was supposed to have stayed in. This incident was really not untypical of the life of the amateur tennis player at that time.

Improving your game and taking on all challengers was the essence of tennis at the highest level. When Billy Talbert, one of the best doubles players in the history of the game and a fellow Cincinnatian, first invited me to go to Europe as his doubles partner in the spring of 1950, I was thrilled, as was my father, who immediately started planning to take out a bank loan in order to cover my expected expenses on the trip.

The loan was never necessary, because Billy had already arranged for the European tournament directors to cover all of my expenses throughout my stay abroad. He said, "If they won't, I will." You can imagine how fantastic that was for me!

After receiving permission from the president of the university to take time off from school, I quickly packed my bags, and we headed for Europe. This first trip proved to be a broadening experience both athletically and socially. My eyes were opened to how people lived outside the confines of Cincinnati, Ohio. I stayed in some fine hotels and ate in wonderful restaurants. Along the way, Bill also introduced me to an incredible array of tennis players and tennis officials, many of whom remain my close friends to this day.

Bill and I ended up undefeated in all our matches, winning both the Italian and French Championships. Although I was later drubbed on Centre Court in my first Wimbledon singles effort, I returned to Cincinnati in midsummer totally changed by the adventure. I had learned that I could hold my own against the world's best players. Now that my competitive appetite was whetted, I couldn't wait to get back to Europe to play again.

On that first trip, Bill and his wife, Nancy, taught me about the social graces. They believed in me as an athlete and as a friend and were among my biggest boosters. In the ensuing years, they invited me to stay in their apartment in New York City. Here I could live rent-free and train with Bill at some of the local tennis clubs around the city.

Looking back on those penniless days, I see how different it was from what many young players go through today. I think the reason players from my era ended up such a close-knit fraternity was that we all shared the same love for the game and the same struggle as we moved up in the ranks. In the truest sense, we were amateur sportsmen, a phrase that certainly is outdated today in a sport that has a yearly purse in excess of $30 million. Tennis is what threw us together, but it was the shared experiences of traveling and playing in matches here and abroad, solely for the love of the game, that linked us so tightly. I will always be indebted to Bill and Nancy for all that they have done to help me, both as a struggling athlete and as a friend.

3
Why American Pros Are Losing Dominance

C ompetition on the pro level today is fierce, more so than when I played, mainly because the talent pool is so much larger. Junior tennis is also much more carefully organized. There are many tournaments for young players to compete in, and much more individual coaching is available. With all of this extra attention, one would naturally expect to see positive results when these juniors move into the collegiate ranks and later to the pro level.

Surprisingly, this is not happening in the United States. The junior ranks seem unable to feed the ranks of the top professionals, and America no longer has a long list of blue-chip pros who can win the major tournaments the way they used to. Tennis fans want to know how this could have happened.

Based on numbers alone, we ought to be ahead of the rest of the world in producing champions. We have the most sophisticated pool of sports and fitness resources available. Exercise physiologists and biomechanicians are constantly testing and exploring new means of developing strength and endurance in all athletic endeavor. But none of this seems to have helped tennis much.

Americans are routinely getting knocked out of the major tournaments and have even been shut out of the finals of their own U.S. Open for two years running. Normally, big servers do well on the DecoTurf II at Flushing Meadow, just as they do well on the fast grass courts at Wimbledon. Americans Tim Mayotte and Brad Gilbert, who both have a good serve-and-volley game, along with Jimmy Connors, had their chance for glory in New York, but they just weren't up to the competition in 1986. In 1987 Gilbert did get to the quarterfinals, while Connors advanced to the semis before he ran out of steam.

Today, with the presence of so many good Swedes, West Germans, Czechs, a few Spaniards, and some South Americans, the chances of winning are diminished considerably for Mayotte, Connors, and Gilbert.

Being a very talented player no longer guarantees you a spot in the final four of any tournament. If you have the misfortune not to be "on," or if you're not mentally primed to win, or even if you have one bad set in a tournament like the U.S. Open, your opponents will pounce on you immediately and send you stomping off to the shower before you even know what hit you.

What's ailing the American program? This is a question people are asking me more and more. Nowadays, Americans have low computer ratings and appear to be getting knocked out early in many tournaments, whether it be the grass at Wimbledon or the clay at the Stade Roland Garros. (I was the last American to win the French Open, and that was in 1954 and again in

1955.) Being in the Top 10 world rankings is a major accomplishment, but unfortunately in this country spoiled by so many number 1's in the past, anything but the top spot, currently held by Ivan Lendl of Czechoslovakia, is viewed with disdain.

If you've been unaware that Americans haven't been faring too well on the courts, perhaps the following facts will make you ask, "Hey, what *is* going on here, and what can we do to change things?"

The ATP computer rankings for 1987 show that American players have 10 of the top 40 positions in the standings. Although they may be doing well in tournaments, Americans certainly aren't winning any of the major tournaments the way they used to. In 1986, for example, no American man made it to the semifinals of the U.S. Open, something that hadn't happened in 16 years. For that matter, no U.S. male made it to the semis of any Grand Slam event in 1986.

Since 1978, when seven of the Top 10 players were Americans, there has been a steady decline of top-ranked Americans. The Top 10 included six Americans in 1980, five in 1981, four in 1982, and three in 1984. In 1987, Jimmy Connors, an old-timer at 34 years old, and John McEnroe, 28, who plays a limited schedule, were the only two remaining in the top 10 world listing.

Among the women, the situation isn't much brighter for Americans. In 1980, five Americans were in the Top 10 world chart. By 1986, there were only Chris Evert, Pam Shriver, Zina Garrison, and a fourth, if you count Martina Navratilova, 29 years old, who lived in Czechoslovakia most of her life before becoming an American citizen several years ago.

Serious doubts about the prospects of U.S. tennis arose again in 1987 when Boris Becker and his West German mates defeated the U.S. Davis Cup team of Tim

Mayotte, John McEnroe, Ken Flach, and Robert Seguso, knocking them out of the 16-team world group for the first time in the history of Davis Cup play, sending them to the lower-echelon zone play for the 1988 season. If American tennis doesn't find a new savior soon in the form of a reincarnated John McEnroe or a youthful Jimmy Connors, the United States may end up in zone competition for quite some time.

In 1988, the opening Davis Cup Zone I match for the United States could be played in Peru on heavy clay courts against a team that wants to get into the elite 16-team World Group. Like Paraguay, the country that defeated the United States in 1987 on its home courts with the help of fans who pelted the Americans with coins as they played, Peru could have noisy and aggressive spectators who will do their best to make trouble for the North Americans.

As the U.S. players start slipping out of the Top 10 rankings, the Europeans and South Americans are stumbling over themselves to grab the vacated spots. Their play is obviously sharper and better than ever, and their competitive appetites have been whetted by the $35 million in prize money now available on the men's tour.

I'd like to see Americans back on top in tennis, not just out of patriotism, but because I think that the sport of tennis gets hurt when no American or an Australian is in the top ranks. These two countries are rooted historically in the game, and their mere presence in the finals of a major tournament is enough to stimulate people around the world to play the game, go to tournaments, and watch the matches on television.

The lack of an American in the finals of the 1986 and 1987 U.S. Opens severely hurt the CBS television ratings. American sports fans have always liked to cheer for the home team, but in 1986 they had only Ivan Lendl of Greenwich, Connecticut (by way of Czechoslovakia), and Miloslav Mecir (also of Czechoslovakia), and in 1987 only Lendl and the Swede Mats Wilander. So the fans missed out on the usual "us against them" or "good guy against bad guy" scenario. The result was that millions of people chose not to watch the U.S. Open on TV those years.

There are three main reasons American pro tennis players aren't winning the big matches. First, the professional game of tennis is naturally cyclical. Over the years, players from one country have dominated most of the tournaments, only to be replaced several years later by players from another country. The United States is presently in a "down cycle" and has been for several years. But using history as a guide, I don't expect them to stay down for much longer.

Driving this cycle is the nature of tennis—an individual game with few national ties. The popularity and success of one player in a country is often enough to set off a wave of tennis participation. The cycle moves into an upswing. But because the sport is so dependent on the continued success and charisma of that player, the wave of participation can die out just as quickly as it began. Then the cycle swings back down.

A look at the record books will give you a clear idea of the cyclical nature of tennis dominance. Frenchman René Lacoste and his fellow Musketeers, Jean Borotra, Jacques Brugnon, and Henri Cochet, ruled the tennis world in the latter part of the 1920s and early 1930s. Fred Perry, England's all-time great, won Wimbledon three times in a row and dominated for a part of the 1930s.

In the 1950s, Dick Savitt, Vic Seixas (my doubles partner), Gardnar Mulloy, Budge Patty, Art "Tappy"

Technically sound tennis fundamentals learned as a youth, the ability to rigidly adhere to a good nutritional and physical training regimen, and the still continuing desire to seek improvement in his game are factors that have contributed to keeping Czechoslovakia's Ivan Lendl at the top of the world rankings.   PHOTO COURTESY OF AP/WIDE WORLD PHOTOS

Larsen, Ham Richardson, and I battled Australia's best in the finals of most of the majors. Aussies Frank Sedgman, Mervyn Rose, Ken Rosewall, Lew Hoad, and Rex Hartwig, also were successful in that period.

In the 1960s, the Aussies came back with the likes of Neale Fraser, Rod Laver, Roy Emerson, Fred Stolle, Tony Roche, and John Newcombe. These players walked away with most of the hardware and the winner's checks.

By the 1970s, American stars Arthur Ashe, Stan Smith, Jimmy Connors, John McEnroe, and Vitas Gerulaitis recaptured the Top 10 rankings, grabbing their fair share of the major tournaments. But as these players retired or simply got older and lost their speed, no other Americans of prominence stepped in to fill the void in the late seventies and early eighties.

So far, much of the 1980s belongs to the Europeans. Although the United States has some good performers in Brad Gilbert and Tim Mayotte, we can depend on the aging Jimmy Connors and the distracted John McEnroe less and less. They just aren't the dominating players that the Europeans are proving to be.

A second cause of the poor results of Americans is that too many of them are spoiled. They no longer want to put out the extra effort that's needed to bring about consistent winning.

It seems ironic that so many young Americans who are pursuing a disciplined career in tennis should also have been spoiled rotten during their developmental years. Far too many parents take their youngsters to their clubs for private lessons and then drive them back home again. Whenever Junior needs a new racket, it appears instantly. Tennis sneakers? Which brand do you want this week? These kids often have their own stereo, color television, telephone, and, when they get

older, their own car. Since their parents have given
them everything, far too few junior players really learn
what it is to sacrifice or to work hard for anything. This
me-first attitude is directly responsible for their poor
showing on the court.

As this generation of American juniors gets older and
moves up the tennis ladder, many never find out what it
means to fight, to discover, and then to expend that last
20 percent of physical and mental effort that will bring
them victory. It's that extra 20 percent that marks the
difference between a good player and a consistent big-
time winner. In contrast, many of the European players—especially those from Iron Curtain countries, who
have everything to gain by performing well—have a
"hungry" attitude.

The desire to see improvement is what drives most
people to excel. But for a talented young player from
Czechoslovakia, Bulgaria, Romania, or the Soviet
Union, this desire is being supplanted by other incen-
tives that American kids have no inkling of: a desire to
better themselves socially and a burning desire to es-
cape the sameness of life in their country, perhaps even
a chance to get out to a free-world country.

A third reason American pros aren't faring too well is
that, as young players coming up through the ranks, far
too many have received poor tennis instruction and
consequently can't play well on all surfaces. At the same
time, East Bloc governments (governments that historically have looked upon success in sports as a positive
reflection on them and their way of life) have been providing top-flight instruction free of charge. Consequently, players such as Larisa Savchenko and Andrei
Chesnokov of the Soviet Union are starting to creep up
into the world rankings, fighting for a shot at the top
prizes in some of the biggest tournaments in the game.

The inferior tennis instruction that many American

kids receive stems from an emphasis on winning. Parents and coaches drill into juniors as young as 12 years old that they have to win, now! And if they don't win, then they're losers, not only on the court—and this is the most devastating—but in life as well.

With the importance of winning elevated so high, American kids are then taught fundamentals and game strategy to bring about winning. But with this overemphasis on beating opponents in their age group, they're seldom taught how to play on different surfaces and rarely instructed in an all-court game, a style of play that's more physically demanding (and will result in youngsters making mistakes and losing matches now and then), but one that will suit them well as they get older.

A good gauge of how well junior players have been taught over the years is to see how many tournaments a formerly successful junior wins after moving up and entering the pro ranks. The record hasn't been very impressive of late. One former junior who was obviously short-changed by his early coaching is 22-year-old Jimmy Arias.

Arias cut his teeth at the Nick Bollettieri Tennis Academy in Bradenton, Florida, opened in the mid-1970s by Nick Bollettieri, a former marine paratrooper. This facility became the first of the many live-in tennis compounds for promising junior players that have sprouted in this country.

Arias had a lot of early success in tournaments and turned pro when he was a skinny, 15-year-old 120-pounder. He had a big forehand but was a counter-punching specialist who rarely ventured in from the baseline. By the time he was 18, he had advanced to the semis of the U.S. Open, eventually finishing out the year at number 6 in the world.

Life was looking good for Arias on the pro circuit, but

before long his opponents started capitalizing on his glaring weaknesses, and it's been downhill for him ever since. The basic problem is that Arias hasn't improved his game much since he was 15 years old. His current ranking is 36 in the world, and it probably won't get much better unless he drastically overhauls his style of play.

In my opinion, this is a reflection on the teaching methods of Nick Bollettieri, Arias's one-time mentor. Has any player come out of Bollettieri's academy a more complete player than when he or she went in? I can't think of one.

This may have something to do with the "grind 'em out" approach to tennis that some academies seem to take. Instead of teaching proper stroke mechanics, these academies have students spend a lot of time hitting thousands of forehands or backhands in their own particular style or fashion—even if that style is technically incorrect. This is a critical mistake and leads to a lot of technical problems later on.

There is a classic way to hit a forehand and a classic way to hit a backhand. If you shake hands with your racket handle with the racket head perpendicular to the ground, you have what's termed the classic forehand grip.

Now, if you take your hand and slide it under the racket handle a little bit more, you'll have the Western grip. Problems develop for players who use this grip, because it requires that you develop a "loopy" type of swing à la Bjorn Borg and, to a certain degree, Ivan Lendl and Boris Becker. This means that you'll have to drop the racket head below the flight of the ball and swing up the back of it on a vertical plane, brushing the ball with the strings as you follow through.

Swinging like this will produce what is known as topspin. The ball actually will rotate forward as it travels through the air. The more vertical your swing is, the more topspin you'll produce on the ball. Because of the physics involved, a ball hit with topspin will drop more rapidly, landing short on the court, accelerating upward at the opponent. Topspin can be a formidable offensive weapon if used properly, because it will give you safety over the net (more clearance) and helps work an opponent back down the court. But whenever you hit with excessive topspin, you have less power in your shot than you would with a flatter stroke. A word of caution: the more spin that you put on the ball, the less speed you'll get. If you're looking for more speed (pace), don't hit with so much spin.

When you do decide to put spin on the ball, try not to make it excessive. A ball with some topspin that easily clears the net and lands deep in your opponent's court should be your goal. Leave excessive spin to the pros who are willing to put in the practice time to incorporate it into their game. Anyone else who tries excessive spin is asking for trouble.

The Western grip is suited for a baseliner but doesn't work very well for a volleyer because of the grip mechanics involved and its overemphasis on topspin. Don't use Western grips; there aren't many people who win with them. Approach shots are very difficult to make using this grip and many short shots you take to set you up for the first volley end up going into the net. In the pro ranks today, Boris Becker could be an exception to the rule, but he's the only one I see who uses this type of grip, yet still volleys well.

The best volleyers have a grip that's somewhere between a forehand and a backhand. This way, when they have to make quick volleying exchanges, they don't have to be concerned with changing their grips in order to make their shots. In most situations, they wouldn't have time to do it anyway.

Stroke mechanics aside, over the years I've found that many of Nick Bollettieri's better junior players are one-dimensional. Sure, they have good groundstrokes, but that's only one aspect of the game. None has a serve or volley worth mentioning, with the exception of Paul Annacone (who happens to have less than reliable groundstrokes), and this list includes Aaron Krickstein, Carling Bassett, Jimmy Arias, and Kathy Horvath, each of whom was once considered a potential bright light on the pro circuit while still in his or her teens. To date, none of these players has improved much since becoming a pro.

Yes, Nick Bollettieri and other academy directors can say that they have developed pro players. And yes, these pros are now making a decent living on the tour. But many of these players are not consistent winners. For this reason, I'm not a fan of most tennis academies and would be very selective in recommending one to any junior player.

If I were coaching a one-dimensional junior, I would focus all of my energies on developing the player's weaknesses. A vast improvement would result from teaching him or her how to volley, how to serve, how to combine good groundstrokes with an all-around game that mixes the pace with some lobs and drop shots. Unfortunately, some coaches let their young players work only on what they happen to do best instead of trying to sharpen their weak points. This, of course, is only human nature. But it will eventually limit the player's full development, something that U.S. players sadly find out when they come up against a well-schooled European or South American player.

To use an analogy, if you got home and saw two

phone messages waiting for you, one from your friend and the other from the Internal Revenue Service, who would you call first? The serious-minded person would call the IRS without hesitation to clear up any problem immediately. The not-so-serious person would call his or her friend. It's easier and certainly a lot more fun.

Most people want to do what's most enjoyable. What's enjoyable, however, is not always the right thing at the time. This principle applies to tennis practice. If a player has a big forehand but a shaky backhand, it will be easier (and more enjoyable) to go out to pound that forehand instead of working on the weak backhand. The player may feel good because he's working hard, but a clever opponent will eventually expose this glaring weakness.

A good player spends much more time on the weaker parts of his or her game before drilling on strengths. But not many young pros are making this effort, most likely because they're making too much money already with their limited success on the tour. No doubt, many ask themselves, "Why work any harder than I have to?"

By erroneously holding up Jimmy Arias as an example of a junior player who went on to make bundles of money on the tour, tennis academies continue to attract a stream of juniors every year. The young players live together, go to school, and play tennis under the watchful eyes of their coaches, all in hopes of someday following in Arias's footsteps. Yet do they really want to be limited to a baseline game?

In the past, all the top players have worked to improve their skills and technique. Whenever there was a break in the season, Don Budge—acclaimed as the best in the world in 1937 and 1938 and a player many feel was the best ever—would work on his forehand until he felt it becoming the equal of his devastating backhand. Martina Navratilova, the most dominating woman's player I've ever seen, has added a topspin backhand to her repertoire. Mats Wilander of Sweden has tried to work his way out of the topspin/baseline style of play that enabled him to win the French Open at 17. He's since added a one-handed backhand and learned to serve and volley effectively. Because of these extra efforts at improvement, Wilander has won the Australian Open three times (twice on grass, more recently on their new rubberized surface) and the French Open again on clay. He also reached the finals of the U.S. Open in 1987, losing to Ivan Lendl in a marathon match that went for almost five hours.

Practicing effectively is all part of being the best in the world, as opposed to being 40th in the world. Unfortunately, by the time far too many juniors eventually realize this, it's either too late to change or they're unwilling to put in all the work needed to improve sufficiently.

The result of this misguided and ill-conceived strategy is that, although kids may be successful in the 12s, 14s, 16s, and 18s with a Western forehand, a two-handed backhand, and highly developed baseline game that will earn them a national ranking on slow surfaces only, they'll never go on to achieve their full potential as tennis players. Once they get to the pro circuit, they'll be ripped apart by Europeans who are well-schooled and possess fully developed serve and volley offenses, in addition to having the necessary groundstrokes.

European players have another advantage over their American opponents: they've grown up on clay courts, which have taught them patience and how to use the entire court when they play. Consequently, they've developed an analytical style of playing, moving their opponents around the court to create openings just as you would a chess piece.

This early training on the slow surface has stood them in good stead. When they later move on to the much faster hard courts, the better European players are able to adapt to the quicker pace, using the techniques learned on clay, blending them into their new serve-and-volley attack. As a result, they prevail against American players, who rarely see clay courts anymore and know only about life on the baseline of a hard surface court.

Coaching top American junior players is no easy task, I assure you. It takes a strong-willed instructor to be able to get a 14-year-old who is already cleaning up the competition with his or her limited baseline game to practice with a serve-and-volley attack. But it's this type of forceful, even-handed, mature adult guidance that kids need the most if they're really going to remove their flaws and be able to take on international competition.

I've always felt that junior tennis could be improved by eliminating most national rankings and by phasing out the national tournaments for the lower age groups. Without the focus on developing a national ranking based on beating one's peers, a youngster can work on developing a more rounded game that would be of more benefit as he or she got older.

My idea of a good junior tennis program would include teaching and working with players on all the strokes, with the main goal being to make sure that the player becomes an all-court specialist. This means that the player would be taught to be effective playing on clay, a much slower and more demanding surface, as well as to have a game that's suitable for a fast surface such as cement or grass. In my estimation, the player who has a full arsenal of strokes and a game suitable for fast and slow surfaces has a chance to go all the way to the top and remain there.

Getting more Americans on the top of the tennis world will take some serious reeducation. Parents will have to learn not to push their kids so hard, so young. Coaches will have to broaden the scope of their instruction to include all facets of the game. And the United States Tennis Association, singled out by just about everyone as the reason for the current poor performance of the American pros, will have to move to the forefront. It should assume a more aggressive role by making access to tennis just as easy as it is to baseball or football, helping in the discovery as well as the nurturing of new tennis talent in this country.

Of course, the absence of U.S. players in the top ranks is not some sort of tragedy. But by being aware of the situation and taking steps to correct the problem, I'm sure that Americans will be back in the Top 10 before long, pushing the European and South American athletes to even greater lengths. I'll be happy to sit back and enjoy those matches, because oh, what battles those will be!

4
Taking Care of
Tomorrow

Where will the next generation of John McEnroes or Jimmy Connorses come from? Getting
a good crop of young tennis players is basically a matter of luring enough athletically talented kids
to the game by the time that they're eight or ten years
old and then keeping them interested in playing. Just as
a young boy will proudly say, "I'm a baseball player," or
a girl will say, "I'm a gymnast," we need millions of
youngsters who'll stand up and say, "I'm a tennis
player." Once this occurs, we'll have a good talent base
on which to build. This can happen if we provide youngsters with plenty of coaching and ample court time, and
if we make them tournament-tough just as we do in
baseball, football, and basketball.

Tennis as a sport needs to make a good sales pitch to
the youth of this country. Modern tennis is hardly a
throwback to the genteel days where the rich played a
set or two at their fancy club and then sat around sip-

ping gin and tonics on a hot summer afternoon. Although too many people still think of tennis as a sport of the rich, in 1968 when the game began allowing pro and amateur players to compete for prize money, it left all the blue-bloods behind and effectively opened the doors to anyone talented enough to play.

Professional tennis is a fierce, competitive athletic contest in which talented players can make an awful lot of money. When people marvel at the high salaries commanded by football, baseball, and basketball players, they should realize that the better tennis players make as much or even more money than the top pro athletes from other sports. And tennis players are just as athletic and competitive as athletes in other sports.

Even so, few young people are playing tennis compared to baseball, for example. For more kids to get into tennis, the game has to be demystified and made more accessible—just like baseball, football, and basketball. This will happen when kids find out that trying to ace their opponent is just as normal as trying to belt a home run or throwing a long bomb in football for a touchdown.

As it stands now, American tennis loses far too many of its top athletes to the big three: football, basketball, and baseball. Had he been raised here, the multitalented Ivan Lendl probably would have been a point guard in basketball, while Boris Becker might have spent his high school and collegiate career crashing through the line as a running back in football. Martina Navratilova would have been a high-scoring guard on the U.S. Olympic basketball team and most likely would have ended her sports career playing basketball in Italy or Japan.

One thing is certain now: tennis, if it's played at all, is a game that most Americans pick up only after their other sports careers are finished. This situation must change if we're going to get enough top players into the sport.

When I played my tennis in the 1940s and 1950s, the sport was just as competitive, but in many respects it was certainly a lot simpler than it is today. We never had any special managers, agents, or, for that matter, any money. If you liked to play tennis, you played it when you could. If you loved tennis, you played it all the time and tried to earn state, regional, and national rankings for yourself.

Later on, when I went on the amateur circuit and played in tournaments, all of them except for the Big Four Grand Slam events were generally played at small clubs that swelled with about 3,000 spectators when we came to play. The postmatch party was a good way to pick up a free meal before we hit the road for the next week's event. If we hadn't been able to stay in someone's home for free, which saved us plenty of money, we couldn't have made it financially.

The game has certainly changed dramatically. In mid-December 1967, the British Lawn Tennis Association (BLTA) unanimously voted to make the next Wimbledon tournament open to amateur and professional player alike. For the BLTA, this was a bold move. The association had packed stadiums for their Wimbledon Championships regardless of inclement weather and a field diluted of talent (most top players at this time had already turned pro and couldn't play Wimbledon). Risking the ire of the governing International Lawn Tennis Federation (ILTF) by declaring Wimbledon to be open could have cost them sanctioning as a viable tournament. But the Brits, fed up with the "shamateurism"— the payment of huge sums of appearance money to amateur players—felt that it was about time to get all the top players in the world, amateur and professional, to play against each other, with prize money offered to the participants.

By the following March, the concept of open tennis was unanimously approved in a hastily called meeting in Paris at the headquarters of the ILTF. The next month, Mark Cox, an amateur, defeated Pancho Gonzales in the first round of what was the first sanctioned open tournament, the British Hard Court Championships. A new era had begun, a new page turned in the tennis history book.

Open tennis brought with it steadily escalating purses and world-wide television exposure, which have made household names and instant millionaires out of kids barely into puberty. Encouraged by the growth in the game, the tennis federations of Czechoslovakia, Sweden, and other countries have built and emphasized their own development programs for junior players. These federations actively search out their young, gifted children and help them to move up the ranks with instruction, financial assistance, and encouragement.

In Czechoslovakia, being a good player can bring extra perks not available to the average citizen, such as better housing, more food, a television set, and travel outside the Soviet bloc. The result of all this government assistance is a group of superior players who are now making their presence felt in the professional tennis world.

Discovering tennis talent in Czechoslovakia is not left to happenstance as it has been in the United States. The Czechs, like the Soviets, West Germans, and Romanians, have long believed in sports science and the discovery and development of talented athletes. Czechoslovakian youngsters are first introduced to organized paddle tennis at six years old, and as they get older and more proficient, they move on to regular tennis. The Czech tennis federation has 90,000 junior tennis players registered to play, and there are well over 500 tennis clubs in the country, 90 percent of which have ongoing programs for younger players. Spread out over this country of 15 million citizens are seven regional training centers staffed by tennis federation–sponsored coaches. Promising youngsters are regularly sent to these centers for tennis training and competition. Each year, the top 60 juniors are selected to attend the youth sport center, where they live, study, and train year-round along with Olympic-caliber athletes from other sports.

Many West European countries also have lately adopted a more direct approach for discovering and supporting young tennis players. In France, organized tennis tournaments are regularly scheduled throughout the year in order to uncover new talent in the seven- to eight-year-old group. The gifted youngsters who are chosen are then offered eight free lessons in one of the 30 regional training sites that the tennis federation maintains throughout the country. In addition, the youngsters are provided with free instruction, practice time, and tournament play once or twice a month.

Sweden, a country of only 8 million citizens, has long been producing top players but without benefit of any highly developed and stratified system. Sweden seems to succeed on the international level because Swedish youngsters have such easy access to tennis courts and instruction that they start to play automatically. The country has 1,000 local tennis clubs, many of which charge only $10 for a year's play for junior players. Short-court tennis, a modified version of the game, is also popular with the younger players, and this encourages them to move up to the regular game when they get older.

Sweden has no formal training centers, but the tennis federation does sponsor week-long camps for the better players three to four times a year. The country has a national team, and the Swedes who play on it seem to be very supportive of each other, something you rarely see with players in this country.

Merely emulating the national junior development programs of Sweden and Czechoslovakia will not automatically make Americans world beaters, too. That may take some time, as the case of Australian tennis points out.

Before Pat Cash's stunning Wimbledon victory over Ivan Lendl in 1987, there had been no bona fide Australian world champion since John Newcombe 15 years earlier. What makes the current Australian dearth of top players so surprising is that more people are playing the game recreationally in Australia than ever before. Also, more money and time are spent with junior development than when Australia ruled the tennis world in the 1950s, 1960s, and early 1970s.

Still, Pat Cash is the only player to have made any impact in all this time. It will certainly be interesting to see whether Cash's Wimbledon success helps bring out more top-notch Aussies and launches a new cycle of world dominance. My guess is that it will.

With U.S. tennis fortunes crumbling in the early 1980s, tennis fans and boosters started clamoring for change. In the wake of the 1986 and 1987 U.S. Open and 1987 Davis Cup misfortunes, the United States Tennis Association (USTA)—the official governing body for amateur and recreational tennis in this country—under its new president, Gordon Jorgensen, finally decided to take some positive steps to bolster America's slumping professional tennis forces. The USTA Committee on Player Development was formed, co-chaired by J. Howard "Bumpy" Frazer, a regional vice president of the USTA, and Arthur Ashe. The committee members are Jack Kramer, Stan Smith, Billie Jean King, Dennis Ralston, Gene Scott, and I. This committee will attempt to devise ways to bring more young players from different areas of the country into the game and eventually to make the United States again the dominant tennis nation.

The United States certainly has an abundance of great athletes. Unfortunately, relatively few of these talented and gifted performers have been attracted to tennis. The USTA has come up with a $6.5 million plan entitled "Taking Care of Tomorrow," which should change all this. Beginning in early 1988, this multifaceted program will entail not just looking for players in the usual places (private clubs, fancy prep schools, colleges, and the warm-weather states), but also in the inner city, which has traditionally turned out many of our top basketball, football, and baseball stars but virtually none of our tennis players. It would be exhilarating to discover and help develop a future Magic Johnson and see his raw athletic talents adapted to the skills of tennis. "Taking Care of Tomorrow" should make this possible.

"The key to long-range improvement in the quality of junior tennis is the involvement of Americans from all economic levels," says Jack Kramer, the 1946 and 1947 U.S. National Champion and member of the International Tennis Hall of Fame.

When you think about sports, you can easily come up with names of prominent black superstars like Willy Mays, Bill Russell, Oscar Robertson, Wilt Chamberlain, Jackie Robinson, Hank Aaron, Gayle Sayers, Julius Erving, and Reggie Jackson. But in tennis, the only names that come to mind are Althea Gibson, who won the women's singles at Wimbledon in 1957 and the U.S. singles title in 1957–1958, and Arthur Ashe, who won the first U.S. Open title at Forest Hills in 1968 and later the Wimbledon title in 1975. Zina Garrison and Lori McNeil are only now beginning to make rapid strides.

The odds seem to be stacked against blacks, Hispanics, and inner-city youngsters being part of the next wave of American tennis stars. If an inner-city boy or girl likes tennis and shows any signs of promise, the child's family seldom can afford the coaching needed for advancement to the next levels. What then happens is what has been happening for decades. The boy or girl switches to basketball, baseball, or football, where competition is plentiful and the coaching is free of charge.

As history has shown, it takes more than a Gibson or an Ashe to get blacks to play tennis in significant numbers. Currently only Chip Hooper, a 6'7" powerful serve-and-volleyer, has made it to the upper ranks. He has since dropped back in the standings and now mainly concentrates on doubles play. More positive signs have appeared on the women's side. Zina Garrison of Houston became the first black woman since Althea Gibson to break into the Top 10. Lori McNeil, Garrison's close friend from Houston, is right behind her.

These developments are thanks to the personal efforts of John Wilkerson, a 48-year-old black tennis coach at the public courts in MacGregor Park in Houston, who first saw some sparks of talent in two 10-year-old girls who came to him for free lessons. Garrison and McNeil have been his personal projects and have made great progress together since then. At the 1987 U.S. Open, McNeil, seeded 11th, beat Zina Garrison and then followed this up by knocking off Chris Evert in the quarters.

McNeil's victory was especially noteworthy for two reasons. She stopped Chris from reaching the semis for the first time in 16 years, and she caught the attention of the crowd with her powerful net rushing and skillful shot selection. In historical perspective, McNeil's victory had to rank as perhaps the biggest win for any black player since Arthur Ashe beat Jimmy Connors at Wimbledon in 1975.

Tennis can be a lifetime sport. But for many athletes, the major stumbling block, according to some observers, is the paucity of tennis courts in inner-city neighborhoods. However, this notion oversimplifies and avoids the real issue. Few tennis courts are in any neighborhood in any urban area in this country. In the city, public tennis courts are often found in easily accessible parks and are generally well-maintained by the municipalities. People of all races and ethnic backgrounds can play on these courts. Still, minorities don't seem to be attracted to the game. Why? I think the cause goes back to the origins of the game of tennis in this country.

Unfortunately, tennis has always been regarded as an elitist sport. Playing tennis was expected of people with affluence, breeding, and a certain background. As a result, those who were being ostracized economically, socially, or racially were restricted from various arenas and country clubs and were never recruited to play the game. Today, the remnants of these antiquated ideas still linger culturally.

Tennis is, in reality, a fantastic physical activity, a great competitive game, and a sport one can pursue independently. The only prerequisites to play are a racket, good coordination, and a burning desire to get the ball over the net as much as possible. It's the perfect lifetime sport. Tennis equipment is minimal and affordable for virtually everyone. Tennis courts are available, though admittedly less so than basketball courts and baseball diamonds.

However, what is really needed in order to get great numbers of inner-city kids to play tennis is a proper introduction to the game, followed up with free and regular coaching. This is where the U.S. Tennis Association can take positive steps to expose more minorities to the game. It's the USTA's responsibility to educate, not just to perpetuate what already exists. By working with city parks departments, by putting backboards in playgrounds, by organizing and sponsoring local tournaments, by inviting and paying local teaching pros, even leading American pro players, to come and give clinics in the parks or local clubs, the USTA will certainly expose many more youngsters to the game.

John Wilkerson understands that this is what's needed to spur black participation in tennis, only he's not so sure the USTA will follow through. "How many facilities staffed with teaching pros will be going up in the inner city?" he asks. "If the USTA isn't willing to sponsor a facility there, then they're not addressing the problem. The kids will come to play and you'll get champions if there are available facilities and proper coaching given. This is why in sports other than tennis there are so many great black athletes."

I don't believe that things just happen randomly. They happen within the context of social and economic circumstances. By making its presence felt in the inner city, the USTA will certainly help make the game accessible to all Americans, ensuring the sport not only of new players, but of success in helping to put tennis right up there in popularity with baseball, football, and basketball—its proper spot as an outstanding American pastime.

When the "Taking Care of Tomorrow" master plan

Heroes play a big part in developing and maintaining an interest in participating in sports. When American professional tennis players are able to give more of their time to offer instruction and encouragement to younger players on a sustained basis, we'll start to see a bigger tennis playing base being built in this country. This photo was taken after Frank Sedgman, Ken Rosewall, Pancho Segura, and I *(left to right)* finished up one of the tennis clinics that we often gave for kids in conjunction with Jack Kramer's pro tour. PHOTO COURTESY OF THE TRABERT ARCHIVES was first announced at a press conference during the 1987 U.S. Open, some grumbling was heard from current and former pros. Said Jimmy Connors, "Why did they wait so long?" Even Arthur Ashe admitted that the plan was about four years overdue. "That's when we could first see the bottom falling out of the American system after John McEnroe and Jimmy Connors," said Ashe.

The ultimate goal of the USTA plan is to attract more young players to tennis and to keep them playing the game, and I'm all for that. When most American adults look back to Little League, many have fond memories of playing a sport that was well-coached, well-organized, and just a lot of fun. In its own way, that's what "Taking Care of Tomorrow" is intended to bring about for tennis in a few short years. Here's a closer look at the program and some of its major points:

- Local-entry programs will be a major first step to entice youngsters into playing tennis. A USTA/National Junior Tennis League is already in place, with over 175 chapters and 250,000 youngsters taking part, but under the new USTA plan, 1,000 programs will be set into operation in as many public parks and schools as possible in order to provide sound developmental training. At these same facilities, "Excellence Programs" would help train the better players and establish local teams and leagues for players up to 18 years of age.

- The second level of the plan will be to help young players reach their maximum potential. This will entail eliminating all national rankings and tournaments for the 12s and 14s, thereby allowing younger players to practice and develop their game instead of worrying about winning. History has shown that you don't have to be a top-ranked player this young in order to make some impact on the game later on.   In the l6s and 18s, national ranking and championships will continue, but in order to develop an all-court and all-surface game, greater emphasis will be placed on clay court competitions.

- Level three is aimed at the very talented players. The USTA will establish 100 training centers, each one no more than a 12-hour drive from a young person who plays. At the centers, the most promising 2,000 players will be invited to come for short stays, where they will receive instruction from leading coaches and former players.

- Four to six USTA regional training centers will provide training and counseling for the most promising juniors. National training camps will also be held in which the best players will come to work out together as one team called the USTA National Team. During the year, all national team members will compete in all international tennis play, including the Junior Boys' Davis Cup, Junior Girls' Wightman Cup, Junior Men's Davis Cup, and Junior Federation Cup.

The most promising members from the USTA National Team will be included on the U.S. Davis Cup and Federation Cup squads. The Davis Cup is a yearly international team tournament for men only that's been played since 1900 (when Dwight Davis, a recent Harvard graduate, put a $750 silver bowl up as a prize). The Federation Cup—named after the International Tennis Federation (ITF) in Paris, the governing body of the sport—is an international team tournament for women and was first staged in 1963 at the 50th anniversary of the ITF's founding. Unlike the Davis Cup, which requires a series of elimination matches that are played around the world throughout the year, Federation Cup play is held for teams at one location for one week.

- To train a small number of the best prospects, the USTA will select several boys and girls as young as 15 years old and take care of all their training needs for three to five years, as long as they agree to follow USTA guidelines and keep up with their schoolwork. These players, regardless of their national ranking, will be taken to Europe and South America to give them experience on clay courts and to pit them against the highest levels of international competition available.

- For a few top young professionals just starting out on the pro tour under the umbrella of "Taking Care of Tomorrow," a traveling coach will be provided for at least a year.

"We want to win the Federation Cup. We want to win the Davis Cup. We want U.S. citizens to win the U.S. Open," said Bumpy Frazer, one of the major architects of "Taking Care of Tomorrow" and a man who's confident that once the plan is implemented and in place for several years, these lofty performance goals will be within our grasp. "We have the best facilities, the best coaches, and certainly the best athletes in the world," added Frazer. "It's about time we put all the ingredients together in some logical, more accessible fashion."

If all of these goals are eventually realized, the United States should once again have athletes playing in the finals of the major tournaments. The USTA can now certainly provide the means to victory by identifying promising players and assisting them in many ways as they learn the game.

This new plan does not guarantee that there will be American winners on the pro circuit. Tennis champions, like all great athletes who have come before, must be highly motivated. The USTA can assist them in perfecting their skills, but the athletes themselves must be willing to push themselves to the top. Only time will tell whether enough young Americans really want to dedicate themselves to this goal.

5
The University of Life: Developing the True Scholar/Athlete

For the most part, the Americans I played tennis with on the amateur and pro circuit were college educated. They were knowledgeable in a lot of areas other than tennis and could and would carry on conversations about varied subjects. After a tournament in India during the late 1950s, I remember sitting down with a few of the players and Indian Prime Minister Jawaharlal Nehru and having an enjoyable, wide-ranging conversation. Nehru was also an athlete and sportsman, as we discovered in our meeting with him. When he was a boy, his father had sent him to England to be schooled. While there, he played tennis regularly and later participated in the Queen's Championships, the tournament that takes place the week before Wimbledon. Nehru, India's first prime minister and a man who played a critical role in setting a course for India after its independence from England in 1947, was also a well-known scholar and an internationally respected leader. It was a rare and unforgettable treat to meet with him.

Most of all, the players I knew on the tour were witty, which certainly helped break up our daily routines. Pancho Segura, the little Ecuadorian, was by far one of the funniest. Once I traveled with Pancho by car on Jack Kramer's pro tour, and we ended up in Marseilles, France, on a hot summer afternoon. Pulling up to a street corner, we spotted a *clochard* lying comfortably on the sidewalk under a broad shady tree with a rolled-up newspaper under his head and a half-filled bottle of *vin rouge* clutched tightly in his grime-streaked fist. His clothes were tattered, and he appeared not to have a care in the world as the soft summer breeze tickled his face. Segura leaned over and studied the man for a moment and then said to me, "Think he has any tax problems, Tony?"

We drove a lot of miles on the Kramer tour, with players sharing the driving duties. Pancho Segura would, of course, try to curl up in the back seat, claiming that he didn't know how to drive, or, when pressed, that he really wasn't a good driver. Finally, on one long trip, from Dallas to Tampa, we forced him to take the wheel while we were still within the city limits of New Orleans, so we could catch up on our sleep. This was a serious mistake. I awoke slightly more than an hour later to find that Segura, while exhibiting good driving habits and obeying all the speed laws, was somehow still on the road going around New Orleans.

"I told you I had trouble driving," he said as I sent him to the back seat. I don't remember Segura doing much driving after that.

Although most of my contemporaries were witty and had broad interests, not everyone was. I recall one instance in particular when I was in India. We had an open day on the schedule, so I decided to look into chartering a small plane so we could all go see the Taj Mahal, which was only about an hour away by plane. I talked it up among the guys, telling them that it was one of the most beautiful buildings in the world, a mausoleum built for the emperor's wife in the 17th century. To my amazement, nobody wanted to go with me. Instead, they spent the day lying around the hotel playing cards.

Another time, we were in South Africa for a tournament and had some free time on our hands. A few miles away was Kruger National Park, one of the world's largest wildlife sanctuaries, with almost every species of game in Africa living within its borders. I thought it would be great if we went over to see the animals. This time a lot of the fellows thought it would be a good idea, too, so we all agreed to turn in early that night.

The next morning, the hotel concierge came knocking on our doors at 4 A.M. to get us up in time. When he came to Pancho Gonzales's room and knocked, there was no reply. After repeated knocking, Gonzales finally woke up and shouted through the door, "If I wanted to see any lions, I'd buy myself a ticket and go to the circus. Now beat it before I get even more annoyed."

Those of us who went to Kruger attended a special barbecue held in our honor that evening at the home of a South African tennis official. Our host was amazed at how dumbstruck we seemed as we recounted our stories of seeing the wild animals close up in their own environment. Having seen elephants and lions only behind bars at city zoos, we found it quite an experience when these wild beasts approached our Land Rovers, sniffed the tires, and then moved on by as if we weren't even there.

After we were finished telling our tales, our host put his drink down and asked whether our guide had pointed out any fighting elephants. When we told him that the only elephants we had seen were lolling around the local watering hole, seemingly at peace, he told us about a visit to the park a few months before, when he found two elephants engaged in a bitter battle. A larger, older elephant was being gored by the tusks of a younger, seemingly stronger elephant, who was fighting to take over the herd from the old timer.

"This is a rare sight, so get photos of this while you can," said the guide. "Once the younger elephant defeats the older elephant, the older one will be so humiliated in front of the herd that he'll limp off into the brush and commit suicide. We'll try to follow him and take some more photos."

Elephants committing suicide? I had never heard of such a thing and interrupted our host. "How would an elephant do himself in?" I asked.

"Well, we never got to see it that day," said the man, "because our truck broke down, and we were unable to keep tracking him. But according to our guide, the suicidal elephant usually gets down on his two front knees, sticks his trunk up his rear end, and then blows his brains out."

Everyone roared in laughter as I was caught—hook, line, and sinker—by that one.

It's certainly a misconception on the part of tennis fans today who think that all pro tennis players are well-mannered and well-educated or, since they travel so much, possess an appreciation or even a basic understanding of the different cultures they're exposed to. Many of today's tennis pros haven't gone to college, while most of those who did attend failed to graduate. The last American player with a college degree who won a Grand Slam singles title was Arthur Ashe, and he graduated from UCLA in 1965.

The primary education of today's pros has come from what they've been able to absorb from around the tennis courts. But believe me, from what I've seen as a TV commentator, this is not the place where you can expect to pick up much of anything except how to improve your game.

A college education is a powerful tool that most players choose to forgo, opting instead for a stab at the pro tour. Sad to say, it's a bad gamble that far too many pay for later.

Many parents ask me for advice about their tennis-playing children. These talented kids get monthly allotments of equipment from manufacturers and are courted by agents who fill their minds with stories about the great life they'll have as pros. Many parents are torn between sending their Johnny or Mary to State U. or just letting them loose on the tour. With rare exception, I encourage parents to send their kids to college, especially since no junior player is a cinch to make it on the pro tour anymore. Take Billy Martin as a typical example.

Martin cleaned up the junior circuit in the early 1970s and then accepted a scholarship to go to UCLA. Martin never had a good "concluder" shot that could put people away when things were getting close; instead he relied on his overall consistency and his extreme mental toughness. Still, Martin did very well on the tennis court, winning the NCAA Singles title in 1975, his first year at college. He had the makings of a good pro, or so he thought when he abruptly left school after winning his NCAA crown.

Martin's abilities were certainly good enough against junior players and later against the best collegiate stars. But this carried no weight whatsoever with the big boys. Although fundamentally a sound player, Martin

Shortly after Jimmy Connors won the National Intercollegiate Championships in 1971 while a student at UCLA, he left college and joined the pro ranks. His 105 singles titles in the ensuing years—the most ever won by anyone—are a testament to his skills. But players of Connors's ilk come along only once or twice in a generation, and I still recommend to parents that they send their tennis-playing child to college for four years instead of letting them turn pro right away.

was battered by tour vets who had seen many Billy Martins come and go over the years. In the end, Martin had sacrificed three years of schooling at UCLA, years that possibly would have helped solidify his game as well as provide him with a college degree.

I always ask parents what their son or daughter plans to do once his or her legs give out. What will happen if their child develops back problems, bursitis in the shoulder, tendinitis in the elbow? What happens when their child finds out that he or she really doesn't have what it takes to sustain a pro career? Not only does a player need good tennis skills to make it, but a thick skin as well in order to put up with all the psychological distress players are subjected to on the tour. Not all young people have the maturity to face or accept these prospects at such a young age.

From what I've seen, kids are much better off going to class and playing a tough NCAA tennis schedule in the fall and spring than they are crisscrossing the country in a van trying to qualify for pro tournaments. A college degree is a valuable asset. Playing tennis in college instead of going on the tour gives young players the opportunity to get four years of no-cost education (which can translate to $80,000, depending on which school they go to), while working on the fine points of their game with a good coach.

Of course, there are a few rare exceptions to my "stay in college" dictum. I'm a prime example, but a special case, as you will see. After returning from my summer tour in Europe in 1951, I was all set to enroll again at the University of Cincinnati for my third year. I was drafted during the Korean War, however, and spent the next two years in the Navy, including over one year on the *Coral Sea*, an aircraft carrier. When I was finally discharged in June of 1953, I went into training for tennis and two months later won the U.S. singles title at Forest Hills. I've been involved with tennis ever since and never returned to the University of Cincinnati to get my degree.

I didn't go back to Cincinnati for two reasons: All of my classmates and friends had graduated while I was away in the Navy. Furthermore, since it was clear that I could hold my own against the top players in the world, the time had come for me to go out and play them regularly.

Instead of pointing to the McEnroes, the Grafs, and the Beckers as examples of players who joined the pro ranks early, parents should ignore them completely. There will always be a few gifted young tennis players who are ready for the pro life without finishing or even starting college. Roscoe Tanner, Jimmy Connors, and John McEnroe came to the pros at 18 and made an instant and long-lasting impact on the game. However, these are but rare exceptions. The list of young players who left college for the glory of the pros and had no impact whatsoever is much longer.

The average pro career is thought to be about seven years long. Whether you turn pro at 15 or graduate from college at 21 and then turn pro, it doesn't seem to make much difference. But the odds of having a more successful pro career and subsequently an easier transition into something else (a good J-O-B) once tennis is finished are stacked heavily in favor of the tennis player who is a college graduate.

College players are able to mature at their own pace and work on all facets of their game. A good college coach will teach them to play with intelligence rather than impulse. The coach will also try to iron out imperfections in their strokes. College players also gain a sense of confidence that comes from winning consis-

Dan Goldie epitomizes the true student/athlete. A top junior player and later a member of the junior Davis Cup team, Goldie attended Stanford University where he earned All American honors from 1983–86. In 1985 he was the PAC 10 Player of the Year and the following season won the PAC 10 Student Athlete of the Year award. In 1986 Goldie added the collegiate outdoor title to his 1985 indoor title, the first to ever accomplish the feat. Following graduation he turned pro and is currently ranked 50th in the world. PHOTO COURTESY OF ADVANTAGE INTERNATIONAL tently, and this confidence will later bolster them if they decide to go the pro route after graduation.

A younger player who leaves college early and becomes a pro really has only one chance to make it. For me, it was clear that I wouldn't have too much trouble playing the world's best, and it wasn't such a big risk leaving college. Today, it's a risky proposition for almost every young player. Once the door to college tennis is firmly shut behind a player who leaves to go on the tour, the player later has to come up with his or her own money to finish college. Few seem to go back to get that degree.

Many of the foreign players have their games pretty much together by the time they're 16 years old. Just look at Steffi Graf. However, Sweden's Mikael Pernfors needed more time. After failing to gain a spot in the Swedish junior tennis program that was packed with the likes of Mats Wilander, Anders Jarryd, and Joakim Nystrom, Pernfors decided to accept a scholarship to the University of Georgia after first spending two years at an American junior college. It was a good move. Pernfors picked up two NCAA singles crowns at Georgia as well as a valuable college degree.

In 1985, while Boris Becker won Wimbledon at 17 on his first try, Pernfors at 21, college diploma in hand, went to the finals of the French Open in his first Grand Slam effort. He eventually lost to Ivan Lendl 3–6, 2–6, 4–6, but ended up ranked 13th in the world for 1986. It appears that Pernfors has a bright future ahead of him, even without tennis.

Another benefit of college that can't be overlooked is that it exposes youngsters to something besides bouncing balls, locker rooms, and sweat. Sequestered in a university setting, they're able to meet people their own age from different parts of the country. They can socialize and exchange ideas. The simple social graces that they develop here, such as politeness, kindness, and how to interact with other people, will serve them well later on if and when they finally make the pro tour.

Most importantly, college offers them a chance to grow as people. Not much of this happens in the sterile environs of the tennis world. I remember vividly being in Tokyo in 1986 for the Seiko Super Tennis tournament, one of the two major men's tournaments held in Japan each year. It was a quiet night during the tournament and a group of young Americans were spending their spare time driving tiny remote control cars around the chairs of the tennis arena. "We're bored out of our minds," a player said to me when he saw me standing there. "There's nothing to do in Tokyo."

I was a little taken aback by this remark. "Ever hear of a book?" I finally asked. "Why not read, learn something about the city or about Japan. Learn something about the people here and try to find out why they're so different from you."

A blank stare. I tried again. "Did you ever think of getting a map of Tokyo and going out for a walk?" This elicited some shoulder shrugging before he went back to his toy.

The top tennis players travel the world, but not many could tell you anything about the different places they visit. All they do is practice, play matches, eat, and go to bed. "The Eiffel Tower? Umm, let's see. Is it in London?"

6
Life on the Tour

Monte Carlo, Paris, Nice, Milan, Rome, Florence, Hong Kong, Tokyo, Madrid, London. These cities, which are major stops on any traveler's itinerary because of the inherent beauty of the city or the different cultural or culinary delights offered, are also some of the major stops on the men's tournament schedule each year.

Unlike the traveler who can visit these cities at a leisurely pace, tennis players fly in, participate in the tournament, and then get the first plane out, heading for the next city, the next tournament. The obstacles that top tennis players have to hurdle as they circle the globe accumulating winners' checks, computer points, and frequent-flyer mileage are formidable. Jet lag, fatigue, muscle aches, and a host of foot problems brought on by switching from clay to hard court surfaces exacts its own special toll on the body. A player's ability to prepare mentally and physically to overcome these problems has a lot to do with his or her ultimate success as a tennis player.

The pro game now spans the globe, with Grand Prix matches taking place just about every week of the year. Air travel has simplified life in a lot of ways, but it can be grueling if the player lets a tournament schedule get out of hand. Even though the Men's Tennis Council (MTC) requires the top players to compete in a minimum of 14 tournaments each year in order to be eligible for bonus points and the Masters Tournament at the end of the season, almost all choose to play in more, in addition to participating in the Davis Cup, exhibitions, and special events.

Since players choose to play in so many tournaments, they end up flying through more time zones in one season than ordinary people do during a lifetime. It's hardly the glamorous life of a trendy jet-setter, because this hectic travel pace brings on the serious problem of jet lag.

Jet lag is simply the physical and mental changes brought on by rapidly traveling across several time zones. Although many have learned how to cope with its effects, jet lag can humble even the best player in the world if he or she tries to ignore it and then play through it.

Players may be constantly setting and resetting their watches to the new local time, but their body's physiological systems adapt less readily and can actually be hours behind. For a tennis player, this can mean disaster. For example, although a recently arrived player from New York may be penciled in for a morning match at the Foro Italico in Rome, his body may still think it's bedtime back in New York where he finished up in the Tournament of Champions 48 hours earlier. If a player seems to be a step slower than usual or, worse, as if he's

The Point System Explained

While earned prize money is perhaps the most self-evident indicator of how well a player is doing, it's not the primary method used to determine who is number one in tennis. Instead, all pro tennis players are ranked according to the number of "points" he or she has won in previous tournaments over a 52-week period.

These numerical points are awarded by the ATP (Association of Tennis Professionals) for men and the WITA (Women's International Tennis Association) for the women according to a not-so-simple system based on a player's finishing position in a tournament as well as the relative prestige of the tournaments that they've played in. The more difficult the tournament, the more points a player wins. For example, advancing to the second round before losing in a Grand Slam event such as the Australian Open will earn a player more points than going to the semi-finals of a tournament in Nice or Athens.

In addition to the computerized point system used by the respective player unions, there is also another bonus point system in force that's set up by the Nabisco Masters for men and Virginia Slims for women. Their point systems are in effect at all of their sanctioned tournaments and are based on the amount of prize money won by a player. Again, the more difficult the tournament, the more points that are awarded.

At the end of the year the top eight male point winners who have fulfilled their playing obligations to the Men's Tennis Council are invited to play in the Nabisco Masters, an extremely lucrative round robin tournament that's been held at Madison Square Garden in New York. In 1987 Ivan Lendl won the tournament and was awarded a first prize of $210,000. He was also give an additional $800,000 for the bonus points he had accrued during the season. Just like the men, the top women point winners are invited to play in an equally lucrative Virginia Slims World Championship Series, their year-end event, which is also held at Madison Square Garden.

sleepwalking on the court, he usually is. That's what jet lag can do, even to a Top 10 player.

The rule of thumb regarding jet lag is that for each time zone that's been crossed, one day should be set aside for the body to fully adapt. But an adjustment period is unfortunately out of the question for the talented player who makes it to the finals of one tournament and then has to move through several time zones to get to another tournament to play two days later.

Not only are normal sleeping, waking, and eating patterns disrupted by jet lag, but so are more than 300 other bodily functions that occur rhythmically during a typical 24-hour, or circadian, schedule. Fiddling with these natural rhythms can bring on headaches, lethargy, and changes in breathing, blood pressure, and oxygen use. More often than not, trying to play on the center court in Roland Garros when your body says you should be eating breakfast in Los Angeles is a losing proposition.

Todd Snyder, one of the two full-time athletic trainers who tend to the injured players on the men's tour, recalled an extreme case of jet lag that involved Johan Kriek. Several years ago, Kriek finished up an indoor tournament in France, then immediately flew to Australia for the start of another tournament. After his last match, he turned around to fly back to Europe for another engagement. When that was over, he raced to Tokyo for the beginning of yet another tournament. It was there that Kriek's odyssey finally came to an abrupt end.

"By the time that Johan got to Japan, he didn't know if it was day or night," said Snyder, "or whether he was tired or not tired, hungry or not hungry. He was so burned out physically and mentally that he had trouble thinking."

As scheduled, Kriek went out to play his match. But left with only minimal physical abilities because of his globe trotting, he defaulted after three games and then went straight to bed.

Although Johan Kriek's case of jet lag is certainly an extreme one, unavoidable scheduling problems brought on by Davis Cup obligations, tournament postponements due to bad weather, and airline disruptions often expose even the best-intentioned players to jet lag.

Researchers have found that the effects of jet lag vary from person to person. Although a player may seemingly adapt to a new sleeping, waking, and eating pattern in two days, it often can take as long as seven or more days for body temperature and heart rate to return to normal. That's fine when a player is taking part in one of the four Grand Slam events that last two weeks, but in the case of a string of week-long Grand Prix tournaments, each one interspersed with jet travel through time zones, jet lag can pose problems.

In the later part of his career, Vitas Gerulaitis grew wary of jet lag. "Between the ages of 18 and 25, there wasn't a punishment that my body couldn't take," said Gerulaitis, a player on the Davis Cup team in 1979 that defeated Italy 5–0 for the title (I was privileged to be captain of that fine team.) "But later on, if I missed getting a good first night's sleep after arriving in either Europe or Australia, I would be ruined for several weeks after that. Waking up at 3 A.M. ready to start a day can really do strange things to your body."

According to trainer Todd Snyder, what helps most of the players overcome jet lag is exercise. "When players fly to Europe from New York or South America, they try to sleep on the plane," said Snyder. "Even though it's morning when they arrive, their bodies think it's still the middle of the night. A lot of them will go straight to the court and practice in order to get into the rhythm of European time. For the rest of the day, they'll do their best to stay awake and then get to bed early that night."

A player who is really intent on doing well in a tournament will arrive at least four to five days in advance, said Gerulaitis. "This is not only to take care of the jet lag problem, but also to get used to the food and hotel accommodations. 'Careful Preparation' was Bjorn Borg's motto, and he would prepare better than anybody else by arriving early for tournaments and then going into hibernation. I'm sure that this was a big reason why his record is one of the best around."

Although every city that the tour visits has its own charm, before tennis players can take time off to enjoy the sights, they must give first priority to their profession—tennis. A conscientious pro will scout out the new territory, set up a base camp of operations, and secure the position with any necessary backup or equipment. Loosely translated, this means booking court time for practice, making certain that transportation from the hotel to the courts is prompt and dependable, and being sure of proper nutrition and adequate rest. In this sense, top players are truly professional. Once the needs of the job are taken care of, a player who is so inclined can often still find plenty of time for visiting museums, taking in plays, or trying out a new restaurant.

As you can imagine, a normal social life is not always the easiest accomplishment for a world-class athlete. In 1987 Boris Becker experienced a number of troubles with his coach, Gunther Bosch, because the coach said Becker was spending too much time with his girlfriend and not enough time on the courts. Bosch was subsequently fired over this disagreement, and to date Becker hasn't returned to his former level of proficiency.

Having friends to socialize with outside of tennis is

normal, certainly, but this can take players away from the single-mindedness of their career by allowing them to worry about unrelated matters such as whether their spouse or boy- or girlfriend will be bored while they're at practice. If this happens too frequently, players tend to cut workouts short and burn the midnight oil. Instead of turning in and going to bed early to catch up on some rest, some players will opt instead for a late-night supper and some time at a local disco.

There's nothing wrong with having a good time, but it changes the schedule that helped get a player where he or she is in the world rankings. This doesn't mean that a pro should put off a serious relationship or that it's impossible to be a successful player and be married at the same time, or that a player can't have a girlfriend or boyfriend. Jimmy Connors comes to mind as a player who has managed to mix his professional and private life successfully. This is because he has a wife who understands that tennis is not only his livelihood (and a very lucrative one at that), but also his passion. She and their children often accompany Connors to tournaments.

To have a regular social life, a player has to learn to schedule activities appropriately to accommodate career and off-court life. For many players, achieving this delicate balance of tennis with social life is unfortunately difficult and often results in tumultuous romances or up-and-down playing careers.

Being away from home can be lonely for many players, especially the talented teenagers who are now filling up the rankings. However, the money that these youngsters are making enables many, the young girls especially, to have their mothers accompany them to many of the tournaments. Not only does this give them someone to talk to and confide in, but a vigilant parent can also help protect them from the off-court advances they might receive from amorous men staying in their hotel and from some of the amorous women on the tour.

Sex and the sexual preferences among the players are private, off-court matters that I rarely encounter in my tennis reporting. The question of homosexuality and men playing on the tour has come up from time to time in the history of tennis. For example, Bill Tilden was arrested for molesting ball boys, which had something to do with giving tennis its reputation as being a game for the less virile. At one time, people thought that Bill Talbert and I might have been gay because we did so much traveling together and roomed together on the tour. But this couldn't have been further from the truth.

While the question of homosexuality on the men's tour rarely arises, women's tennis—and the women's golf tour for that matter—has for years now been surrounded by rumors of lesbianism. Again, a lot of this appears to be simply rumor and innuendo. People see certain women players together a lot on tour, and they start to assume that because Player X is with Player Y so much, they must be an "item." In fact, as was the case with Billy Talbert and me, their association is often simply one of friendship.

When it comes to social behavior, there is certainly a double standard for male and female tennis players. If a man on the tour goes to a bar or attends a party and meets women, he's labeled a playboy, a stud, or a swinger and viewed in a favorable light. If a woman does the same thing, she's derided as loose or looking for action. To avoid this negative stereotyping, a good number of female players avoid the smoky bar scene and the discos altogether and stick with their female friends on the tour.

The nomadic life of a professional tennis player isn't necessarily monastic, but it can wreak havoc on or at least curtail an active social life. The tour can be lonely, with little chance to meet and spend time with members of the opposite sex. Opportunities do present themselves, however, often at the functions held during the week of a tournament.

Since tennis tournaments are so heavily sponsored by corporations, some sort of party or social function is linked with most tournaments. In many instances, players are expected to attend these functions, either as a matter of courtesy or because of a provision in an endorsement contract. When I was playing, I'd regularly be invited out, but I turned down most of the invitations. I knew what I had gone through to become the best in the world, and I didn't want to jeopardize my chances on the court with an active social life.

At times, of course, it was difficult, almost impolite, to say no. At the Meadow Club in Southampton (Long Island), New York, a great formal dinner dance was always held on the Saturday night before the finals of their big tournament. When I was a finalist, I agreed to come by and put in an appearance at the dance. Once I got there, I'd immediately head to the bar and get a Coke. Later on, when people would come up to me to chat and offer me drinks, I'd hoist my Coke instead. After an hour or so of this socializing, I'd quietly leave and head right for bed. The next day, the bleary-eyed club members I had met the night before would be surprised to see me play so well and say, "Boy, he's good," not fully realizing what I had to do in order to get ready to play.

All of the top players do the same thing today, watching not only what they eat and drink, but also what time they get to bed. They know that too many late nights will only undo all of the practice and hard work that they've invested in their careers.

Although there is now more money, more talented players, and a worldwide schedule of tennis tournaments, the demands of pro tennis have barely changed since I played more than a quarter-century ago. The U.S. Open has moved from the quiet of Forest Hills to the hustle and bustle of Flushing Meadow, and the Australian Championships have gone from grass to a synthetic surface in their magnificent new national tennis center in Melbourne, which also has a retractable roof so play can continue no matter what the weather. But other than that, the game seems to go on as it did decades ago.

The All England Championships outside London at Wimbledon are one of the old standards of tennis that have been impervious to just about everything. Boris Becker, Ivan Lendl, Pat Cash, Martina Navratilova, Chris Evert, and Steffi Graf go about preparing for the matches at this venerable spot pretty much the same way I did back in 1955 when I won my singles title there.

Generally, players arrive in England at least in time to take part in the Queens Club Tournament in London, a grass-court affair held the week before the Wimbledon Fortnight. Queens gives the players a chance to adjust to grass after coming from the slow clay courts at the Foro Italico in Rome and Roland Garros in Paris. These Queens Club courts are later made available to Wimbledon contestants for practice once Wimbledon actually begins.

Wimbledon, like the three other Grand Slam Tournaments, is a two-week event packed with singles, doubles, mixed doubles, over-35 matches, and contests for juniors. Top-seeded pros, assuming they make it through to the finals at Wimbledon, play singles matches every other day. Alternate days are for practice or·rest, unless, of course, players choose to take part in doubles or mixed doubles.

John McEnroe, who won the doubles competition at Wimbledon in 1979, 1981, 1983, and 1984 with teammate Peter Fleming, basically played doubles whenever he could because he didn't like to practice. Doubles was tennis practice for him and kept him away from the relatively solitary work he would have to put in otherwise.

Not all top singles players choose to play doubles. Bjorn Borg, who won Wimbledon five straight times, and Jimmy Connors, who won at Wimbledon in 1974 and 1982, shied away from doubles, concentrating all of their energies on singles. Connors has not always been averse to playing doubles. He made a rare doubles foray at Wimbledon when he teamed up with his pal Ilie Nastase, and together they won the title in 1973.

I agree with McEnroe when he says that doubles is the best way to sharpen your singles game. Doubles helps you concentrate on your service as well as your returns, and all of this equals better singles performance. Doubles also develops your net game. In good doubles, you'll often have all four players at the net. Lots of quick exchanges take place, and they happen much more frequently than in singles. You have to be ever-alert, ready to make reflex volleys, the short punching motions at the ball that often bring victory.

Whether practicing alone, playing doubles, or working out at Queens Club or Wimbledon, players must allow a block of time for travel to and from the different places. London is a beautiful city, but like any other major nation's capital, it has its traffic problems. Since players can't afford to get stuck sitting in a car, they have to make sure that their driver picks them up with plenty of time to spare.

It takes a good 45 minutes to reach Wimbledon from downtown London, where most players' hotels are located. If a match is scheduled at three in the afternoon, players generally try to get their practice in at Queen's at 10:30 in the morning. They then return to the hotel for a training meal, change clothes, and head out to Wimbledon.

Wimbledon is a magnificent sight. A tremendous hustle and bustle surrounds the All England Club, but there's also such a sense of order and decorum that you feel secure enough to relax. Watching the long lines of English fans, newspapers in hand, quietly queuing up for their tickets—which they won't have in their hands for a good three hours at least—gives the place an air of civility that's not found anywhere else in the sporting world.

From day one, Wimbledon has been the most successful of all the Grand Slam events. At any one time, at least 29,000 people are on the grounds of the club, which was built in 1868 and named the All England Croquet Club. The newly refurbished Centre Court stadium now can seat 12,433, with an extra 2,000 spaces reserved for lucky standing-room ticket holders. The tournament is sold out from the first day, and interestingly no rain checks are given. Here in a country where visitors often see more rain than sun, if Wimbledon spectators get rained out the day that their tickets are good, they're simply out of luck.

English fans love their Fortnight, and even though a top male English player hasn't done well here in decades, the entire country seems to get involved, watching the matches at the club or else live on the BBC.

The English are the most knowledgeable of all tennis

fans in the world and, as a result, the most polite. Although nationalistic and ardent supporters of their own players, they're fair toward players from other countries. Of all tennis spectators, the English seem to appreciate the game the most, and they enjoy good play by anyone.

In the locker room at Wimbledon, waiting to be called for a match is like being in purgatory. The desperate desire to win mingles in the recesses of your mind with the thought that you might not. When the locker room door is opened, muffled rumbling comes in from the packed stadium. The small room with its ancient wooden lockers is filled with tension. Players spend a lot of time nervously twisting grips on their rackets, jogging in place, and swinging at imaginary forehands and backhands. This certainly isn't the time for idle chatter. Heads are often bent as players close their eyes and try to envision how they will be spending their next three hours. Later, just before their Centre Court match, the players are taken to a quiet holding area behind the court. When the call finally comes to head out for a match, it's often a relief to be able to get on with actual play.

Whenever a player goes out to play on Centre Court, he or she must turn and bow toward the royal box upon reaching the service line. The first time that I ever played at Wimbledon was in 1950. I was 19 years old, and my first match was to be on Centre Court, pitted against the English favorite, Tony Mottram, a man all of England fervently hoped would become the next Fred Perry and bring back some glory so long missing from English tennis.

I was to be Mottram's sacrificial lamb to get him on to the next round. I walked out onto the neatly clipped grass, bowed in the direction of the royal box, and then,

In 1955 I arrived in London primed and ready for Wimbledon. Her Royal Highness the Dutchess of Kent presented me with the winner's trophy after I defeated Kurt Nielsen of Denmark 6–3, 7–5, 6–1.

to my utter dismay, proceeded to lose horribly.

Until that time, my international experience had been limited to winning the doubles with Billy Talbert on the clay courts at the Italian and French championships several weeks before. Grass was fairly new to me. I had hit my first ball on grass at Newport, Rhode Island, in the summer of 1948, and had tried it several other times before coming to Wimbledon. Even so, I was not comfortable or confident on the baffling green surface. I assure you, Centre Court with a full house watching really isn't the best place to learn how to handle grass.

Wimbledon is like the Super Bowl, the World Series, and NBA Finals all rolled into one. For me, the very thought of finally being on Centre Court was mind boggling. For a young man from Cincinnati out on his first European adventure, everything seemed to happen at once, almost as if I were operating in fast forward instead of normal speed. The Centre Court net looked higher than a mountaintop, and needless to say, I never got my game untracked. Mottram beat me in straight sets 6–3, 6–3, 6–4, and except out of nervousness, I hardly even broke a sweat.

I trudged off the courts a loser, still in a daze. When I looked back over my shoulder at the court, workers were already out there on their hands and knees replacing the divots that I had dug up with my right toe when serving.

After a match, the players head back to the locker room to shower and pack up their things before arranging for a driver to take them back to the hotel. By the time they arrive, it's usually the dinner hour. If they're lucky, after supper they'll be able to relax a little before climbing into bed.

That same year, I also played in the doubles. I had planned to play with Bill Talbert, but since he had never played Wimbledon before, he opted to play with his long-time partner, Gardnar Mulloy, instead. I teamed up with Budge Patty, an American expatriate and a fine singles player who lived and played throughout Europe. In our quarterfinal match, we were to meet Frank Sedgman and Ken McGregor on Court number 1. At the time, these Australians formed the best doubles combination in the world.

In those days, the men's singles final was played on a Friday. Because of the bad weather, however, we'd only advanced to the quarterfinals of the doubles by Thursday. To complicate matters, Patty and Sedgman were scheduled to meet in the next day's singles finals.

Patty and I won our first set 6–4, and as was the custom then, we changed balls and put fresh ones into play. The second set turned out to be a real dogfight, with the Australians not giving an inch. Finally, with the games tied up at 20–20, I asked the umpire if we could get new balls to play with, because the ones we were using were getting heavy and unwieldly. The umpire politely said that it was against the rules to change balls until a set had ended. I asked if we could switch to the balls we'd used in the first set, which had only 10 games on them, and this request was also denied—very politely I have to add.

"What would happen if I proceeded to hit all of the balls we're using now out of the stadium?" I then asked.

The umpire was perplexed and called for the tournament referee. After a conference at courtside, it was finally agreed that we could use the balls from the first set. We finally won the set 31–29.

Sedgman and McGregor won the third set 9–7, but we came back to win the fourth and deciding set 6–2. The marathon match took a total of 5 hours, 40 minutes.

Frank Sedgman was fit and strong and did a lot of

running to keep in shape. In contrast, Budge Patty was slight of build and relied on tennis for most of his conditioning. I used to kid him that physical training for him meant breaking his cigarettes in two and then smoking only half the amount.

Although we had won our quarterfinal match that day, I felt that the long match had killed Patty's chances to win the singles finals the next day against Sedgman. Much to our surprise, Patty played a superb match on Centre Court and beat Sedgman in four sets, 6–1, 8–10, 6–2, 6–3.

An hour after his singles triumph, Patty and I had to play another Australian team, Geoff Brown and Bill Sidwell. Patty was not only physically tired, but emotionally drained, and we lost in three straight, 6–4, 6–4, 6–4.

As a result of our protracted quarterfinal doubles match, the Wimbledon committee decided to institute a rule change for the following year. Balls would no longer be changed after each set, they decreed, but after a certain number of games like all other tournaments did. They've kept up this practice ever since.

Wimbledon is the unofficial world championship for tennis and the goal of any player who ever lifts up a racket. I know of no player who can think of anything but tennis when playing there.

When you're in London, your blinders are on to all other temptations, and nothing can distract you from your quest. There will always be time for museums and theatrical productions (yes, *The Mousetrap* will probably be there another few decades) once the Fortnight is over. For me, this single-mindedness even covered the reading of newspapers.

In 1955 I arrived in London primed and ready to play. I had repeated my 1954 victory at the annual red-dirt battles at Roland Garros and wanted to grab the elusive

Wimbledon crown as well after I crossed the Channel.

"Whatever you do, don't read the newspapers when you're driven from your hotel to the club for your matches," cautioned Jean Borotra, one of the legendary Four Musketeers of France. Five times a finalist at Wimbledon, twice a victor in the 1920s, Borotra had pulled me aside one day in the player's lounge to offer me this advice about reading.

"The subtle movement of the car will be enough to strain your eyes as you read, and this will detract from your concentration for the task at hand," he said in his heavily accented English.

Difficult as it was, I followed Borotra's advice. I figured that if not reading papers had helped him win at Wimbledon, it might help me as well. But I was nervous and really needed something to take my mind off my upcoming matches. I often looked out the window and thought back to my days on the playgrounds in Cincinnati. I'd certainly come a long way since then.

After I eventually won the singles title, defeating Kurt Nielsen of Denmark 6–3, 7–5, 6–1, I found Borotra at the Wimbledon Ball that night and told him that I had taken his advice about the newspapers.

"See," he said with that knowing look of his, "When you want to be a champion, everything you do plays a small yet very important part."

Putting all of the pieces together successfully is what makes a champion. The extent to which a player is able to juggle or manage a household with a spouse and children, have a social life, survive the rigors of international travel, get in practice time, and then cope with or overcome the special psychological problems imposed by the game itself will greatly determine the type of season the player will have. All things considered, many of the players at the top manage to do a pretty good job.

7
Qualities of Greatness: The Men's Game

When it comes to men's tennis, people often say that it's not worth watching any player not ranked in the top 30, because you're just not going to see top-flight tennis. But the fact is the top 100 players are a talented group of athletes who not only exhibit a variety of playing styles, but will, on just about any given day, turn in a remarkable performance.

Collectively, today's top players certainly have one thing over the players who preceded them: they have a deeper, more talented field than ever before. This stems partly from better instruction, more available court time, more opportunities for tournament play, and the sky-high sums of money that have encouraged more people to take up the game. Today's players are also stronger from improved diet, weight training, and all of those influences we didn't know about before. As a consequence, modern pro tennis players are on the whole physically stronger athletes. Advances in technical

equipment have also enhanced play, first with the introduction of René Lacoste's metal racket, the T-2000, and
later followed with all the other oversized-racket com-
posite blends.

Nevertheless, when it comes down to pure tennis-
playing ability, the top players of any era—and by this I
mean going back as far as 50 years ago to Don Budge—
could still do well against any of today's best performers. The reason is that, while equipment advances
have made some of today's players better by giving
them more power and control, the refinements in racket
technology would not have been lost on any of the top
players who previously wielded wooden rackets so well.
Believe me, Fred Perry, Don Budge, Jack Kramer, Lew
Hoad, Pancho Gonzales, Bobby Riggs, Frank Sedgman,
and the rest would have quickly adapted to the bigger
graphite rackets and been at the top of their respective
world lists. Then, too, these old-time players would
have improved some more with the newer scientific
training methods now used and perhaps benefited from
today's better ideas in "athletic" nutrition.

Many tennis commentators have said that some of
today's male players hit their serves so hard that they
represent a new breed of tennis player. To some extent,
it may be true that Boris Becker, for example, is repre-
sentative of a new breed, but only for his particular era.
Players with booming serves certainly are not new to
tennis. Jack Kramer, Pancho Gonzales, Lew Hoad, and
many others hit the ball pretty hard, and they were
doing it 30 to 40 years ago.

What many tennis fans today fail to realize is that,
while a powerful first serve is an awesome weapon, in
and of itself it's less important than deft placement. The
tennis player receiving serve, like the batter who has to
face a pitcher who throws fast balls at 95 miles per

hour, can learn to return the ball no matter how hard it's been served. In service, what a player can do with that first serve to keep his opponent off balance—being able to disguise placement, or hitting to either forehand or backhand at will—means much more than just being able to blast the ball over the net at 110 miles per hour.

While many of today's players play the so-called power game, check to see whether the player gets a high percentage of his first serves in. If he doesn't get a first serve in, his opponent gets a chance to take a swing at his second serve. This is the best shot a player will normally get, because the second serve comes in slower due to the extra spin, and it bounces up higher. The opponent gets to stand in closer so he can get to it earlier and hit it down to the server's feet.

In evaluating a server, it's important to look beyond the first serve to the quality of the second serve. The server must place this shot well with good depth, good pace, and also some bite or action. This comes from the spin on the ball.

If a player has a strong first serve but succeeds with only half of them and follows up with a powder-puff second serve that really sits up, he's not going to be an effective player. For a pro, a good percentage of successful first serves is in the high sixties, maybe even 70 percent. This doesn't mean that all the first serves are coming in like rockets, either. A player who always hits his first serve with all his might won't be able to get a high percentage of his first serves in.

I think it's better to take some pace off the first serve from time to time so you can get a higher percentage in. Even though the ball may not come in as fast as you're capable of hitting it, your opponent will be standing back farther and will be unsure of what you are going to do. Once you're left with only one ball, your opponent is going to move up a bit and be pretty sure of what you're up to.

In one match last year, Boris Becker had 22 service aces, which led some people to say that, in order to keep the game from becoming too boring—Boom! Boom! Point!—tennis officials should think about moving the point of service back a step or two, or else limiting service to just one try.

This is not a new proposal. When I was a pro, we tried different ways of minimizing the first serve in an effort to make points last longer. But in the end, the better server still served better and usually won the point. When we stood farther back than the baseline to serve, Pancho Gonzales still served better than I did, and the point didn't necessarily last longer either.

On the pro tour, we also tried what we called the "three-bounce rule." The ball had to hit the court three times before anyone could go to the net. Therefore, the serve was the first bounce, the return was the second, the server's return was the third, and then the players could move in as they wished.

In theory, this might help prolong the point by cutting back on the power game, but we quickly figured out that, after one of us served for the first bounce and the opponent returned for the second bounce, we would simply float a ball deep with no pace, a semilob that went back to the baseline. The opponent had to let it go for the third bounce. The floating ball and the opponent's position behind the baseline allowed plenty of time for moving to the net and getting in good volleying position. So much for the three-bounce rule!

Often, more important than skilled serving is the ability to return a hard-hit serve with good pace. Jimmy Connors has no trouble returning hard serves, and most of the Swedish players are adept at it as well. But unlike Connors, the Swedes (except for Stefan Edberg) return the ball with their loopy topspins and keep you on the court for what feels like a month.

This overemphasis on baseline play makes the game boring because it's too one-dimensional. Tennis isn't so exciting when you have to watch a player keeping the ball in play at the baseline, waiting only for the opponent to make a mistake. I like the player who has all the strokes in his arsenal and draws upon them when he sees fit. He can rally when he has to, but once he's given some daylight, he goes to the net and finishes off the point.

Many great players have trod the world's courts over the past half-century. Fortunately, I've had a chance to see most of them play, and at one time or another I've had an opportunity to play against many of them as well. A few players stand out above the rest. These men were great when they played, winning most of the major titles, and their reputation and record of achievement are today used as a measuring stick for those who follow in their footsteps.

Many of the people who saw Bill Tilden play say he was the best player ever to lift a tennis racket. But films of him in action suggest that if he played tactically today the way that he played in the 1920s, he would have trouble beating many players from today's group. I wasn't overly impressed with Big Bill's serve. He was a spin artist, and spin nowadays doesn't affect players enough to throw their games off. Of course, in Tilden's time, players didn't go to the net much, so Tilden was able to stay back at the baseline and use spin.

On a grass court, if a player ever did that to me, I would rush the net, be as aggressive as possible, and make my opponent come up with the ultimate passing shot, which is pretty hard to do because the court causes uneven, erratic bounces and footing is never good. This puts an opponent in a negative situation. Therefore, when a player has the choice, he should go in and make his opponent try to pass him.

When you play someone who hits with excessive spin, you can move up, because a ball with heavy topspin will land short on your court. If you're aggressive and can come to the net often, you shouldn't have too much trouble with a player who insists on spinning from the baseline. A good player will take advantage of the short ball with penetrating approach shots, making volleying easier and more effective.

This assessment is not meant to denigrate Bill Tilden, a player who won seven national singles titles (1920–1925, 1929) and three Wimbledon crowns (1920–1921, 1930). If Bill Tilden had the athletic ability and dexterity that historians say he did, he would have adjusted to today's style of play and perhaps done just as well as he did back in what is now called "the Tilden Era."

Another player I didn't get to see play is Fred Perry. Again, I'm told that he moved as well on the court as anybody in the history of the game. Perry used a continental forehand, which was a devastating weapon, and he used to take the ball on the rise as he charged in to the net. Winning Wimbledon three times in a row, as he did from 1934 to 1936, and the U.S. Championships in 1933, 1934, and 1936, certainly speaks for Perry's abundant talent.

It's been said that Don Budge possessed the greatest backhand in the history of tennis. He would relentlessly drive the ball with that stroke, hitting it with topspin or slice to almost anywhere on the court that he wanted to. Budge was a complete player, not exceptionally fast on the court, but he had solid groundstrokes and a good serve. In 1938 he became the first player ever to win the Grand Slam (victories at the Australian, French, Wimbledon, and U.S. Championships in one calendar year), solidifying his position as one of the true greats of the game.

Jack Kramer was among the top players ever. He had a great first serve, but more importantly, he possessed a deep and effective second serve, which is really the key ingredient in being a good server. Kramer was probably the best volleyer I've ever seen, and was equally good off the ground. He was raised on fast courts, and, as a result, was not as effective on clay. Still, he had the fiery instincts you'll find in all the great competitors, as well as keen analytical skills on the court. Big Jake was the dominating player immediately following World War II. Had he not turned pro shortly after beating Frank Parker at Forest Hills in 1947, thereby excluding himself from further participation in the Grand Slam events, there is no telling how many times Kramer might have won the major titles.

Pancho Gonzales is memorable for his big first serve. The winner of the National Singles title in 1948 and again the following year, Gonzales turned pro in 1949 and won eight U.S. Pro singles and five doubles titles between 1953 and 1969. Gonzales was considered a big player at approximately 6'2", but he moved extremely well for a player of that size. While his groundstrokes weren't spectacular, he was a good volleyer with an especially effective backhand volley.

Australia's Frank Sedgman was an excellent doubles, mixed-doubles, and singles player who won quite a few championships in the late 1940s and early 1950s. Sedgman was extremely fast on the court with a serve that was an effective and reliable weapon. Since he moved so well, he was at the net in an instant, ready to contest

I've always felt that Jack Kramer was one of the top players ever in the history of tennis. Big Jake won the U.S. singles title in 1946 and 1947 and the Wimbledon singles championship as well in 1947 before going on to start his own professional tennis tour. PHOTO COURTESY OF THE TRABERT ARCHIVES whatever his opponent tried to hit back at him.

Fellow Aussie Lew Hoad is another player who ranks as one of the all-time best. Here was a talented player, who, because of a painful back condition, was kept from winning more than he did. Hoadie was strong as an ox. He had a terrific serve and could hit any shot in the book. From time to time, he would lose his concentration, and he didn't always play as well as he wanted. If he did play his best, he could blow his opponent off the court because he had the capabilities of a tennis genius and could rise to heights I could never reach. But the rest of the time, when he was anything but his best and I was playing a high-quality, consistent game, I could catch him and felt that I had a good play on him.

A lot of people say that Australia's Ken Rosewall had the second-best backhand in the history of the game. He was a small guy, 5'7" or so, weighed in at about 140 pounds, and moved very well. Rosewall wasn't a great server, but since he was so short, most of his serves were fairly deep. He showed signs of his great potential early on, winning the first of his four Australian Open singles titles in 1953 when he was just 18 years old.

When I played Rosewall, I outweighed him by at least 50 pounds. He was the counterpuncher, and I was the slugger. I liked playing him because his serve wasn't powerful enough to knock me down as did that of his countryman Lew Hoad. I knew that I always had a chance to get a good piece of the ball and therefore might be able to break his serve. His forehand was a shot I attacked. He hit it crosscourt about 90 percent of the time. I knew this because his grip was close to the Continental, which made the racket face come through early. The ball had to go crosscourt.

When it comes to true tennis greatness, I'd have to rate Rod Laver right up at the top of the list with Jack

Kramer. Laver—all 5′8″ and 155 pounds of him—absolutely dominated men's tennis in the 1960s and early 1970s. A shy and gracious man, this Australian native won the Grand Slam in 1962, the first man to do so since Don Budge first performed the feat 24 years earlier. Seven years later, while playing as a pro, he won the Grand Slam again, becoming the only player in the history of tennis to win the elusive title twice.

Rod Laver would have been a tough opponent for me. Although he was fairly slight, he packed a wallop in his game because he used a lot of wrist in his shots. This gave him additional pace and deceptively masked his shots until the last second. In addition, Laver was technically sound and played consistently at the same high level, match after match. To top it off, he was able to play as well on any surface you put him on. However, if I had had my choice, I would have tried him on clay, which I think was his weakest surface.

While top players today can earn $200,000 in just a matter of weeks on the tour, Laver became the first of the big-time money winners in 1970 when he surpassed $200,000 in yearly tournament earnings. A year later, he also became the first tennis player to post $1 million in career earnings.

With his solid groundstrokes, Sweden's Bjorn Borg would have been tough for me to handle on clay. Still, I would have loved to have tangled with him on grass. I think Borg stayed back at the baseline too much, which left him vulnerable for anyone to come to net.

Borg must have had ice water in his veins when he was on the court. He was in the habit of producing a good shot from the baseline, letting his opponent come to the net, and then assuming the burden of trying to come up with a passing shot of pinpoint accuracy. This was a tough assignment for Borg, mentally and physically fatiguing, and one that became even tougher when he left the normally slow clay surface that he liked so much and tried the same tactics on grass or any other fast surface.

Borg was a battler, and his six French titles and five Wimbledon crowns certainly attest to his talent. Still, even now that he has left the game, he must feel a twinge of sadness, perhaps of frustration, for never having had similar successes at the U.S. Open. Because he never won in New York, he never went to Australia to play on grass in an effort to win the Australian Open title for his Grand Slam. He probably would have won the Grand Slam had he only been able to win the U.S. Open.

Throughout the 1970s and 1980s, Jimmy Connors has been one of the United States' consistently strong players. He won his first of four U.S. Open singles titles in 1974 and won Wimbledon in 1974 and 1982. His apparent weaknesses were his serve and his forehand. Still, Connors is a tough player to go up against, because he is tenacious and usually takes the ball on the rise. He also hits extremely hard.

Jimmy Connors is what I call an "up and down" player. He doesn't have much topspin on his groundstrokes, which makes it hard for him to pull his opponent out of position, so he hits punishing shots with plenty of pace up and down the court, hitting the ball and placing it deep in the corners. Caught in a style of play like this, his opponents have trouble getting off the defensive and trying something of their own.

I would like to have played Jimmy Connors, because I think I could get a swing at his serve. He tosses the ball too far to his right, so much so that his body is in the way when he finally brings his racket through. This cuts back on his power. Still, his relatively weak serve doesn't seem to have bothered Jimmy all that much, or he would have done something to change it by this time. And even with that serve, he's still managed to win 105 tournaments.

While emotionally fragile on the court at times, John McEnroe has certainly gone far with his natural athletic gifts. He has won the U.S. Open four times (1979–1981, 1984), the Wimbledon singles title three times (1981, 1983, and 1984), and the Wimbledon doubles with partner Peter Fleming in 1979, 1981, and 1983. He earned his number 1 world ranking in part by being so talented, but equally by being a perfectionist who is extremely tough on himself. This, I think, is what has brought on most of the on-court tantrums that have marred his brilliant, yet stormy career.

Mac always seems to expect more of himself than is realistic. This often happens to athletes when the game that they're playing comes easily and they don't have to practice a lot to truly develop or appreciate their skills.

John McEnroe hasn't tended to spend a lot of time on the practice court. Since the game is apparently so simple for him, he's often tried tough shots, sometimes low-percentage ones, in matches, expecting to pull the shots off. A player as gifted as McEnroe thinks he can make any shot, no matter how difficult, at almost any time. Making the shot is thrilling, and the spectators roar. But missing is not so good. The attendant mental frustration of missing so many of these low-percentage shots can easily be a tennis player's undoing.

McEnroe's groundstrokes are good, but they can be weak because they lack depth and pace. He's a great touch volleyer, but sometimes less penetrating than he needs to be. Since he started stringing his rackets loosely—in the range of 40 pounds of tension—players are starting to overpower him. If I were working with him, I'd bring the racket tension up to a more reasonable 60 pounds and have him start swinging at the ball more than he is now. He currently just takes a short swing and lets those soft strings of his almost throw the ball back across the net.

I don't know the strategy behind that type of play, but it's easy to see that he's being worked over by the top players that he now goes up against. While he still wins a good percentage of his matches, he doesn't beat the top two or three players consistently enough to regain his number 1 world ranking. The frustration of being unable to do this could be enough to make McEnroe give up on tennis completely.

8
The Women's Game

In 1987 Pat Cash, Australia's 22-year-old tennis player, surprised the tennis world with his 7–6, 6–2, 7–5 Wimbledon final domination of Ivan Lendl. Several days before this, however, he stunned women in particular and the sports world in general with his pronouncement that women's tennis was vastly overrated.

"Women's tennis is two sets of rubbish that last only half an hour," the cocky Melbourne player actually said to *Women's Own*, a British weekly magazine. "The spectators who turn up at events like Wimbledon really come to see the men play. It [women's play] is ruining men's tennis. Whoever negotiates the women's part deserves a medal. Only the top four deserve that kind of money—the rest don't. If there was a women's game and I went out to practice with [Boris] Becker, people would watch our practice game."

Cash's comments were certainly less than diplomatic. But coming from a man who has received a $5,000 fine for bad behavior after one unsportsmanlike incident at a German tournament and who tried to punch out a television cameraman during Australia's 1987 Davis Cup match against Sweden, it really came as no surprise to me that he'd speak before he thought.

The battle lines are quickly drawn whenever someone raises the question of who is the better athlete, a man or a woman. Several years before Cash's recent blunder, Vitas Gerulaitis put his Sands Point, New York, mansion up as a bet that Martina Navratilova, the best women's player, was unable to beat not the best male player at the time, John McEnroe, but the hundredth-ranked male player in the world.

Male chauvinism? Certainly. Martina answered Gerulaitis that she could readily knock off number 100 if she were only given choice of surface. It was Chris Evert, however, who reminded her friend that she felt lucky whenever she got to win a game from her brother, and he was barely a ranked player in the state of Florida. "Martina would lose to the thousandth-ranked man," said Evert at the time.

Evert was right. Women will always have trouble against men because most sports require strength, speed, and quickness, something most men have more of than women.

A personal example: I played Billie Jean King shortly after she beat 61-year-old Bobby Riggs 6–4, 6–3, 6–3 in their much-ballyhooed 1973 "Challenge of the Sexes" exhibition match in the Houston Astrodome. The match attracted over 30,000 paying customers (the largest crowd ever to see a tennis match) and over 40 million TV viewers. I was 43 at the time and not in very good tennis-playing shape, while King was 29 and the number 1 female player in the world. Although I don't really remember the score, I do recall that I beat her without too much trouble.

I didn't make a big deal out of it then, and I'm not going to do that now. My example just illustrates that in most cases a male athlete will defeat his female counterpart. This doesn't mean that I believe women to be any less capable to take part in sports than a man. There are many great women athletes, and they turn in sparkling performances—that is, when they compete against other women.

Physically, women don't have the same body strength as men. They never have and never will. On the average, women aren't as tall as men, so they don't have the reach that men have. In addition, they lack the upper-body strength needed to consistently serve with power and to pound the ball back. And, because they have less muscle mass, they can't run as fast as a man. This is not to denigrate women athletes in any way, but just to state the obvious physiological facts when you compare men with women: the fastest man runs faster than the fastest woman. He can also lift more weight.

The area in pro tennis where women have shown remarkable strength is with their own tour. They've done a fantastic job with a circuit that was first put into operation in September 1970 by Gladys Heldman, the founder of *World Tennis* magazine, and Billie Jean King. King, along with eight other women, each signed a contract with Heldman and was paid a dollar for one week. Thus, they made the break from the men's tour.

At the time, King and other women pros felt that the U.S. Lawn Tennis Association (USLTA) was treating them unfairly in terms of the number of available tournaments they could play in and the amount of prize money that was offered to them. They were right. The National Women's Indoor tournament was the only prize-money tournament for women in the winter, and it offered an unstaggering $2,500 as the total purse, while men were playing indoors each week for purses in the $50,000 range. In the summertime, women fought over $2,500 purses in four summer contests, while the men divvied up an average of $25,000 per tournament.

The USLTA had little to offer women. A few minutes before King's press conference announcing the inauguration of their pro circuit, several high-ranking USLTA officials pleaded with her on the phone not to go along with Heldman. Still, they couldn't offer anything better to change her mind. "I wanted to play tennis every week just like the men did," she said. "I wanted to make money just like they did, too. But since the USLTA had nothing to offer, I was better off trying for something on my own than staying with the USLTA and getting nothing."

Within a year, hooked up financially with Virginia Slims, the cigarette company, women were playing on Heldman's 24-week circuit for $25,000 purses.

If women's tennis was such "rubbish" as Pat Cash seems to believe, then the women's tour certainly wouldn't be as successful as it is today. The tour is not only successful, it's thriving. The Virginia Slims World Championship Series now spans five continents with over 55 tournaments and has $15 million in prize money. A look at the following figures will show you just how close the men and women have become in earning power.

Halfway through 1987, Miloslav Mecir was the leading male player with $755,000 in tournament earnings, while Steffi Graf had earned $667,000 to lead all the women. Stefan Edberg was the number 2 man with $580,000, and Martina Navratilova, who was playing an abbreviated tournament schedule, held the second slot for the women with $490,000 in tournament winnings.

One place where the women have it over the men is with their players union, the Women's International

Tennis Association, and with the strong leadership they've shown over the years. As a body, they speak with a unified voice, and this solidarity has helped in cementing their bargaining positions and building such a strong tour. Chris Evert and Martina Navratilova have each served as president of the tennis association, a situation you don't find on the men's side, because the top men simply aren't willing to give the time.

Equal pay for play was one of the major issues that initially drove the women from the men's tour. Still, women shouldn't get equal pay in the tournaments that they play with men in this country, the Lipton International in Key Biscayne, Florida, the U.S. Open, and the National Clay Court Championships in Indianapolis. This is not just because the quality of tennis isn't the same. Women simply don't have as many quality players in these tournaments most of the time, and they play only two of three sets.

I'm by no means advocating that women's tennis move to a best-three-of-five match format like men's tennis. That would only extend their matches, in too many cases making it that much more deadly to watch. One of my worst nightmares would be if I had to sit through a best-three-of-five women's match played on clay. It's bad enough in men's tennis.

The current paucity in talent in women's tennis is apparent. Playing in the Virginia Slims Championships (a best-of-five-set series since 1984), one woman, Martina Navratilova, has won eight titles in eleven tries. Only once, in 1986 playing against Hana Mandlikova, did any player push her to four sets in order to win the title.

It's probably safe to say that you see fewer good women's matches than good men's matches. That's because although more than 350 women competed pro-

A rivalry for the record books: Martina Navratilova and Chris Evert have dominated women's tennis for a good portion of almost two decades. During one
stretch, they were paired against each other 29 consecutive times in tournament finals. In Grand Slam encounters, Navratilova holds a 13–8 edge.

fessionally in 1986, the talent level of most of these players was not very high. By comparison, the men's field runs much deeper with talent.

Indisputably, the best match during the entire 1986 U.S. Open was the semifinal between Graf and Navratilova that went to a tie break in the third set and had the packed stadium excited throughout. It definitely saved the tournament and bolstered TV ratings. The same thing happened in the 1987 Open when the talented Lori McNeil kept spectators and TV viewers wondering whether Steffi Graf would be able to hold off the advances of one of this country's emerging players.

If women could have matches like these all of the time, or at least a good portion of the time, then I'd certainly say that women should be paid the same as men. But until that time arrives, I don't think the equal-pay dictum really applies.

Unfortunately, women's tennis usually offers blowouts. In the two weeks of the 1987 U.S. Open, the top-seeded women barely broke a sweat in their early-round matches. Of the 16 seeds, only one lost so much as a set in the first round, while in the second round, only one player was knocked off, the remaining 14 advancing and again giving up only one set in the process.

Losers in the first round at the Open received $3,353. This prompted a slightly miffed Martina Navratilova, a player who appreciates talented play, to say to Roy Johnson of *The New York Times*: "They seem to come out of retirement to get a paid vacation."

It's not only in the first rounds that you see blowouts. In her semifinal match of the 1987 Open, Martina needed all of about 50 minutes to dispose of Helena Sukova of Czechoslovakia, the sixth-ranked woman in the world. If you went by past performances, world standing, and the importance of this tournament, you would have expected something special. But this match was so one-sided that spectators were hustling out of the stadium while the match was still in progress, trying to see the junior boys' singles matches being held on the outside courts.

This Navratilova victory only made the absence of depth on the women's tour more apparent. It seems that once you get by the number 6 in the world, the talent drops off sharply. There's seldom ever an upset among the top players in the women's game and hasn't been for years. On the men's tour, upsets occur quite often because with the big serve now a major weapon on fast courts, the top-ranked men are all susceptible to defeat as early as the first round of a major tournament.

When I watch a match, I like to see skill, intelligence, and athletic prowess. Using a lob once in a while to change the pace is all right. But some women players use this forehand, backhand, forehand, backhand routine 30 times a point without coming to the net at least once or trying to move their opponent out of position. Trying to dictate the match and keep the ball in play from the baseline, hoping that the other person makes the first mistake or that her arm cramps up so she has to default, is not the kind of tennis I enjoy.

I'm confident that women's tennis will become much better once more women start to play the complete all-around game as Navratilova does. This, of course, will come once women follow Navratilova's lead and increase their fitness levels and make a serious commitment to their sport by trying to work on their weaknesses.

Whenever you make comparisons in the women's game, all of them have to be made with Martina Navratilova, the one woman who has totally revolutionized tennis with her passion for being as fit as possible. At 30

years of age, she has a career record that says everything: almost $13 million in tournament earnings;
Wimbledon winner (1978–1979, 1982–1987); U.S. Open
winner (1983–1984, 1986–1987); the first person in the
history of the game to win the U.S. Open and Wimbledon in the same year on four separate occasions;
French Open winner (1982, 1984); Australian Open
winner (1981, 1983).

Martina is stronger, is faster, and has a more complete game than any other female player in history. She's
a terrific volleyer, especially with her backhand, a shot
I've yet to see any other woman make as consistently.
She also smashes well and simply moves better than
anyone else before or currently.

If I were coaching a woman who had to face Navratilova, I would take her aside and talk about serve. I
would have her serve a lot of second serves to Navratilova's forehand. Navratilova seems to favor her backhand
because she can take the ball early, hit some underspin,
and quickly come in to the net. Her ball stays down, and
she ends up in perfect volleying position. Point, Navratilova!

If she has to swing at a forehand and then come to
net, she's much more apt to make an error on the approach. If she makes it, at least it bounces up higher.
Her forehand volley is less consistent than her backhand volley as well.

While admittedly singing the praises of Navratilova, I
don't want to make it appear that no other woman
player has contributed to the game. I have tremendous
respect for Chris Evert, the consummate groundstroke
specialist. Looking closely at her game, however, she
clearly doesn't play as well as Navratilova on all surfaces. Her serve isn't a weapon, and she doesn't like to
volley. It's been Evert's strong groundstrokes, along

with her tough will, marvelous concentration, and determination, that have carried her to the top. Selected
as the International Tennis Federation's World Champion in 1978 and 1980–1981, Evert has also won at least
one Grand Slam singles title for 13 consecutive years
(1974–86), a record unsurpassed by any other woman
or man. Well-spoken and well-mannered, Evert will always remain my ideal of a true sports champion.

Billie Jean King was a terrific player and always enjoyable to watch on the court. She scrambled and
hustled and loved to compete. But King and other top
women players from the 1960s and early 1970s like Ma-
ria Bueno and Margaret Court were a notch below Navratilova in talent, strength, or power.

As good as she was, Little Mo (Maureen Connolly,
who, in 1953, was the first woman to ever win the
Grand Slam) couldn't have beaten Navratilova either,
except perhaps on clay. Connolly's serve wasn't that
good, but she made up for it with tenacity. She had
great groundstrokes and would punish her opponents,
taking the ball on the rise and sending it back with
authority. Still, she probably couldn't have stood up to
Navratilova on a grass court. She wouldn't have been
destroyed, because she was too good a player for that to
happen, but Navratilova would have taken advantage
of her serve, as she does so often with the women she
faces nowadays, and then pounced on Little Mo at the
net.

Looking for women who played or were around earlier than Maureen Connolly who could have possibly
had a chance against Navratilova is a mistake. There's
such a tremendous difference between the way women
played the game in the 1930s and 1940s and the way
Navratilova, Steffi Graf, Hana Mandlikova, and others
are playing it today that the eras have actually become

incomparable. Alice Marble, the Wimbledon Singles champion in 1939, once unabashedly confided to Martina, "There's no way I could have ever beaten you even during my prime. You're just too good."

One person who disagrees with me when it comes to Martina Navratilova is Ted Tinling, a courtly, genuinely funny man who's now in his midseventies. Tinling, an old-time international player from England who turned his attention to clothing design after leaving the amateur circuit, has probably seen more women's tennis than any person alive. He claims without reservation that Frenchwoman Suzanne Lenglen, who won Wimbledon six times (1919–1923, 1925), and not Martina Navratilova, was the best female player ever.

I really find Teddy's claim hard to believe, and I keep telling him this whenever I meet him. From what little I can tell from the films I've seen of her in action, Lenglen, who died of pernicious anemia in 1938 at the age of 38, had neither a penetrating game nor a good serve. Navratilova would have quickly capitalized on these shortcomings. Still, Ted persists in his beliefs and won't hear anything I have to say about Navratilova.

Martina Navratilova has been a player of impact, a person the sports history books will record as having dramatically changed forever the tenor of the women's game. She has the best serve I've ever seen in a woman and she tries to overpower and knock her opponent over with it. She also covers the net better than any other woman in tennis. And she lasts. She's prepared to play and has the endurance to stay on the court for as long as she has to.

Future stars on the women's circuit are indebted to Navratilova. They're now abandoning the baseline and the double-fisted backhand and looking to Navratilova for inspiration and technique. Because of her, they're now working harder on and off the court. Martina's legacy will not only be good for the women's game, but eventually as these new faces start to make a name and a reputation for themselves, it will be good for the sport of tennis as well—just as Martina herself has been.

9
So Long to the Bad Boys

T ennis used to have much higher standards of eti-
quette than it does today. In my time, tennis was
very much a "gentlemen's game." Even men who
were not particularly generous off the court were completely professional while playing. Take Pancho Gonzales, for example. I appreciated Gonzales's tennis ability, but I never came to respect him as a person. Too
often I had witnessed him treat people badly without
cause. But he seems to be mellowing a bit.

Born in Los Angeles in 1928, Gonzales was the eldest
of seven children. His father was a house painter and a
strict disciplinarian who didn't hesitate to physically enforce his will whenever he felt the need. And many
times the punishment far outweighed the offense. According to *World Tennis*, once when his father found
out that Pancho had hit his brother in the back of the
head with a rock, the boy was marched out to the garage and hanged by his thumbs from a garage rafter for
three hours.

This type of childhood might help explain Pancho's unfriendly behavior when I met him. I found him to be unapproachable, a loner who kept all of his thoughts and ideas to himself. Sullen most of the time, with a chip on his shoulder as big as a two-by-four, he rarely associated with us on the road. Instead, he'd appear at the appointed hour for his match, then vanish back into the night soon after without saying a word to anyone. We'd all stay around giving autographs to the fans before moving on to the next city. Not Pancho. But on the court, he was totally professional—as well as a fantastic player.

It may be, of course, that players back then were more soundly reprimanded for unprofessional behavior. Any instances of bad behavior—and this included foul language, racket throwing, and other on-court disturbances—were dealt with immediately by officials of the USLTA.

Earl Cochell, a high-ranking amateur American whom I had beaten for the 1951 NCAA singles title, found out just how little bad behavior was tolerated by the tennis establishment. In September 1951, "Tiger" Cochell, a talented player from California with a big serve and unfortunately an even bigger temper, had fallen behind 4–1 after splitting the first two sets of a fourth-round match against Gardnar Mulloy at the U.S. Championships at Forest Hills. Cochell's behavior suddenly became "erratic." A natural right-hander, he played out the remainder of the third set with his racket in his left hand and at times did his serving underhanded. This incited the crowd to start booing him. When Cochell later tried to climb into the umpire's chair to get the microphone and respond in kind, the fans went wild.

Cochell finally lost the set 6–1 and headed to the

changing room under the stadium for the customary 10-minute break. Here he was approached by Dr. S. Elsworth Davenport, a respected long-time tennis official and tournament referee, who told me later that he had only wanted to take Cochell aside and get him to calm down. Before Davenport had a chance to finish his first sentence, Cochell blasted him with a long tirade of salty language that left Davenport stunned and fuming. "I'm no square or prude," said Davenport, who was then in his seventies. "But I'd never been talked to like that in my life."

Cochell stalked out of the room and went back onto the court, where Mulloy proceeded to finish him off quite handily 6–2 in the fourth set. This match proved to be the last organized tennis that Cochell ever took part in. Two days later, Cochell received notice from the USLTA that he was banned from participating in tennis for an "unspecified amount" of time. The suspension wasn't just for his unorthodox conduct on the court (in serving underhanded), but more specifically for cursing at Davenport during the intermission.

Cochell never appealed his sentence. Instead, he vanished from the game and apparently from the face of the earth immediately upon receiving his notice. For more than 30 years, I never heard anything more about him. One day, however, I read in *World Tennis* magazine that Cochell had surfaced in California as a wealthy self-made man who spent all of his time traveling the world with his wife. In a rare interview with a reporter about his ill-fated Forest Hills match, Cochell admitted that serving underhanded was only a tactic of his to help him get by because he was tired and that he became upset that the fans had booed him for using it. In regard to the locker-room incident, Cochell said that Davenport had threatened to default him from the match for his behavior, and this is what set off his foul-mouthed barrage.

Although Cochell wasn't a saint, and in no way do I condone his behavior, he had at least confined his blue language to the locker-room. Today, young millionaires are fined what amounts to peanuts for bad language and for making obscene gestures with their hands and rackets on the court. And this is what I find to be amazing: they're allowed to continue playing and not be defaulted, and they aren't heavily penalized.

During the 1987 WCT (World Championship of Tennis) Finals in Dallas, Texas, John McEnroe was struggling in an early-morning affair against Miloslav Mecir and didn't like the calls of umpire Gerry Armstrong. McEnroe let Armstrong and everyone else sitting courtside know of his displeasure in his typical whining, bad-boy fashion. For this mini blowup, the Men's Tennis Council (MTC) later fined McEnroe $2,000, hardly a sum to dent his estimated $40 million empire and really nothing that would cause him to pause for a moment and say, "Hey, Johnny, I'd better not do this again, or it could be bad for me." Of course, image has never been something John McEnroe has tried to groom and protect. He does not seem to suffer any shame or embarrassment.

After the match McEnroe was quoted as saying, "I'd be ranked 5,000 in the world if I played like he umpires." There was no fine for this public utterance, simply another in a long list of offenses pointing up McEnroe's unsportsmanlike behavior that have marked his brilliant yet all-too-often turbulent career.

Since entering the pros in 1978, McEnroe has picked up almost $10 million in tournament earnings. He has also had to dole out about $80,000 in fines for bad behavior and has been suspended from the tour for this

EXHIBIT C

MIPTC

OFFICIAL POINT
PENALTY SCORECARD

World Open

TOURNAMENT

1/1/87	1st - 32	FRED FAIR
DATE	ROUND	CHAIR UMPIRE

Player(s): John Doe

DEFAULT SCHEDULE	DELAY PENALTY	C O D E	SCORE	DESCRIPTION OF VIOLATION*
	WARNING	K	0-1, 15-15	AS RECEIVER, FAILED TO COMMENCE PLAY WITHIN 30 SECONDS
	Point	K	3-4	AS SERVER, FAILED to RESUME PLAY WITHIN 90 SECONDS
WARNING		L	4-4, 15-30	Yelled, "Shit" after losing Point
Point		O	4-6, 0-2	IN anger, HIT BALL NEAR linesman (ACCIDENTAL)
GAME		Q	4-6, 5-5, 0-15	Called OPPONENT a "ASS"
	Point	K	4-6, 6-5, 15-15	AS Server, failed to COMMENCE PLAY within 30 SECONDS.

Player(s): DAVE Default

DEFAULT SCHEDULE	DELAY PENALTY	C O D E	SCORE	DESCRIPTION OF VIOLATION*
	WARNING	K	6-4, 0-1, 0-30	AS SERVER, FAILED to RESUME PLAY WITHIN 30 SECONDS
WARNING		O	6-4, 2-2, 0-15	Hit Ball out of Stadium, after loss of Point
Point		K	6-4, 3-4, 0-30	AS RECEIVER, argued call and Stated he would not PLAY
GAME		K	6-4, 5-7, 0-30	After INJURY Time Suspension, Player Could not Resume Play after 30 Sec.
Default		R	6-4, 5-7, 5-5	Player Struck Chair Umpire

CODE SECTIONS V

K. Unreasonable Delays
L. Audible Obscenity
M. Coaching

N. Visible Obscenity
O. Abuse of Balls
P. Abuse of Racquets
   or Equipment

Q. Verbal Abuse
R. Physical Abuse
S. Unsportsmanlike Conduct

1/1/87	Fred Fair
DATE	SIGNATURE — CHAIR UMPIRE

* Use Reverse Side for Additional Details of Violation
MIPTC Form No. 3 Revised.
January 1, 1986

behavior a total of six times. This translates to almost eight months of being forbidden from playing in any sanctioned matches. McEnroe has easily surpassed Ilie Nastase, the Bad Boy of the 1970s, as the all-time leader in the Tennis Hall of Shame.

Not only does McEnroe abuse balls, rackets, umpires, and linespeople, but at the U.S. Open in 1983, he actually threw a handful of sawdust at a courtside fan who was cheering too loudly for his opponent, Trey Waltke. For this outburst, McEnroe was sued by the spectator (who happened to be a high school tennis coach) in a Long Island court for $6 million, a suit that was eventually dismissed.

An incident in McEnroe's third-round match against Bobo Zivojinovic in the 1987 U.S. Open easily stands out as the worst behavior I've ever seen, not only on the tennis court, but in all of sports. Just before McEnroe's major eruption in the fourth game of the second set against the Yugoslav, several of Bobo's shots had landed close to the line or right on the line and had been ruled good by the linesman. This had Mac fuming. Serving at set point, he then missed an easy forehand volley, a sitter, a shot he should have made without even thinking. But he didn't.

With the score then at deuce, McEnroe missed another volley and yelled over to Richard Ings, the umpire for the match, "Was that point important enough? It was only set point for me."

McEnroe obviously was annoyed because he had wanted Ings as chair umpire to have overruled the linesman on the previous close baseline calls. When he hadn't, Ings went on Mac's hit list.

McEnroe got the game back to deuce, but then he double-faulted and followed it up with a backhand volley that went into the net, making it 5–4 in games for Mac.

Since turning professional, John McEnroe has picked up almost $10 mil-lion in tournament earnings. It's too bad that he's paid out a portion of these winnings in fines for bad behavior, and has been suspended from the tour a total of six times, which translates into almost 8 months of not being able to play in any sanctioned matches.

During the 90-second changeover, McEnroe started up with Ings, a 22-year-old Australian who is one of the five permanent traveling umpires hired by the MTC. "Can't you see anything? That call cost me the damn set. . . . It was over, completely over, and you can't see a damn thing."

For this outburst, Ings levied a warning, which angered McEnroe even more, prompting him to let loose with a barrage of four-letter words that easily would have had him defaulted from the match if Ings had been able to hear him over the crowd noise. I certainly heard every word of it, because it was all picked up by our CBS television microphones at courtside.

Ings assessed McEnroe a penalty point for his obscene language. Later, Ken Farrar, the Grand Prix supervisor who was at the match and who later reviewed the game tape, hit McEnroe with a $5,000 fine for this specific outburst. "Verbally," said Farrar in announcing his fine, "it ranks as one of the worst incidents I've ever seen during my eight years as tour supervisor."

McEnroe played the next two games of the second set without further incident, but while he was changing his shirt at courtside with Zivojinovic leading 6–5, he began yelling at Ings again. Ings, however, made it clear that he had no intention of carrying on any conversation, and it was then that McEnroe turned his attention to the CBS technician holding a microphone near the net. He let loose with a string of profanities, and for this was assessed a game penalty.

It's amazing that a young man who publicly professes such love for his wife and two children could scream out references to oral sex and unnatural acts within earshot of parents and their kids sitting at courtside. How would McEnroe like it if someone stood in front of his wife and children and said the same things that he did on the court? Being upset in tennis is no reason for vulgarity.

McEnroe has always been a crybaby on the court. If you ever watch one of his matches, you'll see that he'll have a lot of arguments with the umpire or linespeople. Richard Ings was in the chair the day after the McEnroe-Zivojinovic match, and there was not one argument. What does this prove? Do umpires become so incompetent all of a sudden when they get to a McEnroe match? I don't think so. Now and then, they might miss a call, but they certainly don't miss 20 of them as McEnroe seems to think. Mac will put his hands a foot apart and show the umpire that the ball was that far out when, if anything, it may have been out a fraction of an inch.

Mac has a way of creating problems for himself. Even if a linesman does miss a call, what is a player going to do about it? The rule book states that if a linesman makes a "clear mistake," the chair umpire must overrule it "promptly." The rules also state categorically that the chair umpire may "never" make an overrule after an appeal by a player.

World Series umpires sometimes miss calls. NBA refs sometimes miss calls, even in the finals. That's because they're human beings. McEnroe still hasn't been able to understand this about tennis officials. He misses more easy shots every match he plays than linespeople miss calls . . . and this was true even when he was the best player in the world.

Proper behavior is taught at home by parents who care about their children. In the eyes of my father, a man who during the Depression lost every penny he had, bad manners were worse than total lack of money. If I had ever acted on the court the way McEnroe, Jimmy Connors, or Ilie Nastase have, he would have

forbidden me from playing—not because I had embar-
rassed myself on the court, but because I had embar-
rassed him along with the rest of my family. It's up to
parents to nip this type of disruptive behavior in the
bud when their children are young. And then the
teachers, the coaches, and the tournament directors
have to follow through and enforce good behavior on
the courts.

People often say to me that tennis really needs players
with antics like Nastase and McEnroe. They claim that
domination of the game by such supposedly staid and
boring players as Ivan Lendl, Mats Wilander, Stefan Edberg, and Miloslav Mecir leaves pro tennis completely
lacking in any spirit and excitement.

I disagree. Over the years, tennis has had too many
fine ladies and gentlemen as champions for me to believe that swearing and making obscene gestures are a
necessary part of the sport. This type of crude behavior
doesn't add "color" to the game. If you look at the pro
golf tour, you won't see any similar antics, yet the popularity of the tour is at an all-time high. Any flair, any
"color" in the game, should come from the artistry the
players exhibit on court with their tennis skills, from
their interaction with the crowd, and from their person-
ality, which shows up off-court in television and print
interviews. "Color" does not come from such adolescent
behavior as yelling at linespeople or making lewd gestures.

If I were in my prime and playing someone like
McEnroe, Nastase, or Connors, the charter members in
Court Chaos, I would have come to a clear understand-
ing with them long before we ever got to the court.

"Look," I would have said to each one of them, "If you
think you're good enough to beat me with your racket,
then good luck to you. But if you try to pull any of that

funny business on me like constantly protesting calls and psyching linespeople, I'm going to get you. I'll get you on the court if I can, or I'll get you back in the locker room."

Players who act up need to be put in their place immediately, if not by the umpire, then by the opposing player. Once when Nastase was playing Clark Graebner, Nastase started fooling around during the match, and this proved to bc a big mistake. Graebner simply stepped over the net and started to come after him. Nasty did a version of the Romanian Backpedal and escaped quickly without suffering bodily harm. His delicate psyche was upset, however, and a few games later he defaulted, saying that because Graebner had threatened him he was too shaken and couldn't go on any longer.

For his latest transgression at the U.S. Open, John McEnroe received a two-month suspension levied by Marshall Happer of the MTC and an additional $10,000 fine for having surpassed the $7,500 fine limit players are allowed for a 12-month period for the second time. Is the MTC finally getting tough with bad behavior? Not tough enough. Mats Wilander, the complete opposite of McEnroe in court deportment, was fined $5,000 by the MTC. Wilander's transgression? Missing a pre-tournament press conference to help hype the 1987 WCT Finals in Dallas.

To make the punishment really fit the crime, players should not only be fined more money than is now currently levied, but they should also be prohibited from playing tennis exhibitions and making money during that period of suspension. Also, players should be disallowed from playing in the next Grand Slam event. For example, if the transgression occurred in the fall, the player wouldn't be allowed to play the Australian Open

in January. The second time, the player would be prohibited from playing the next Grand Slam event, which
would be the French Open. Only when the MTC takes
strong measures like this will all pros really sit up and
take notice about their court behavior.

My penalty recommendations, though not currently
in the rules, would carry considerably more bite than
McEnroe's penalty of missing two months of what was
actually the slack time on the pro schedule for him.
During this forced layoff, McEnroe was allowed to play
in as many non–Grand Prix events as he could fit into
his schedule. This meant that he would have to pass up
the Swiss Indoor Championships and their $40,000
purse for the winner, as well as a Grand Prix event in
Arizona, which pays $46,000 for first place. Instead Mac
played in an exhibition event in Atlanta in October of
1987 and walked away with $150,000. This was cer-
tainly a nice payday, but it may have come at the expense of McEnroe's tennis skills; as a professional tennis player grows as an athlete, he can only truly test his
skills in the competitive environment offered by the
tour.

Some tennis followers felt that McEnroe's latest suspension would not only cause his computer ranking to
drop, since he wasn't able to defend two of his Grand
Prix titles in that time, but that it might even knock him
out of tennis for good, since he wouldn't have the desire
or mental concentration to keep in shape during this
layoff. Taking a liking to the life away from the court
might finally be what will keep McEnroe away from the
game permanently, just as it did for Bjorn Borg when he
retired from the game at 26. Ivan Lendl has already
remarked in the press that he was surprised to see how
much Mac's game has deteriorated since his 6½-month
sabbatical from tennis in 1986, and that it would be

John McEnroe was surprisingly receptive to coaching when I had him on my Davis Cup team.

best for McEnroe, if he wants to be remembered as a great champion, to leave tennis for good now instead of staying around in the lower echelons.

It's not McEnroe who will suffer if he leaves the tour for good, some tennis fans have told me, it's the professional game of tennis and the fans who will feel his loss. I really don't think so. Arnold Palmer was a tremendous golfer with a worldwide following. When he retired from the tour, they didn't stop holding the Masters just because Arnie's Army was disbanded. When Ted Williams retired from baseball, the Red Sox didn't lie down and die. Granted, John McEnroe is fun to watch as a tennis player. He's a fiery, gifted, competitive athlete with a tremendous arsenal of shots. He can sprint to the net and make phenomenal volleys. His groundstrokes are solid. He makes things happen on the court with his vast imagination and doesn't just try to keep the ball in play as some other players do. Yes, this talent will certainly be missed. But McEnroe's raging, uncontrollable temper and boorish antics, which have detracted far too much from what has been a brilliant career, will never be missed. McEnroe has no one to blame but himself for this. He's written his own chapter in the tennis books, and unfortunately it's not a particularly nice one.

As upset as I am with some of the behavior a few players exhibit on the court, I'm equally perturbed by behavior that I see off the court. In the evening following his loss to Ivan Lendl in the 1986 WCT Finals, I saw Stefan Edberg in the lobby of the hotel. I was to emcee a charity banquet and was dressed in my tux. I approached Edberg and complimented him that, even though he had lost, he had played a brilliant match.

Edberg probably didn't know who I was, but nevertheless I was standing in front of him, and I had just spoken to him. He didn't say a word, though. As a matter of fact, he just stared over my shoulder with a disturbed look on his face as if I were wasting his precious time. I swiftly turned and walked away with a sour taste in my mouth. I was upset by Edberg's nonreaction, of course, but not surprised. Edberg's antisocial behavior is not an isolated case. I've witnessed numerous instances of rudeness from other players as well.

If tennis players can't thank someone who's just praised them for their performance, if they don't have enough class to acknowledge someone who has spoken to them, then it points out that we in the professional tennis community have a serious problem that's only going to get worse. For a sport that is so tightly linked to corporate sponsorship (as opposed to pro sports that rely on spectator ticket sales for revenue), this could be very bad news. It doesn't take much to ruffle the feathers of a corporate bigwig. An executive will call a meeting of the board, and as quick as you can say "service ace," will recommend that the company drop tennis sponsorship and search for new PR opportunities.

The worst-case scenario would be for several of the players to upset some of the major sponsors and then have them pull out of tennis. If this happens—and it's quite possible, since we're talking about image (which is something a good number of the players need to work on) as well as performance—professional tennis would go through some hard times.

Pro golfers have it over their tennis-playing counterparts in so many ways. To get a PGA card, which allows a player to participate in the PGA-sanctioned tournaments, each golfer has to qualify based on skill, and then attend classes to learn, among other things, the history of the game of golf. Here the players find out how pro golf developed. They're told how Ben Hogan won the U.S. Open in 1950 and earned a few hundred dollars. They're told how Gene Sarazen, Byron Nelson, Ben Hogan, Sam Snead, and Jimmy Demaret helped develop and nurture what has become the multimillion-dollar tour that they are now trying to become a part of. In essence, the PGA qualifying school shows aspiring golfers that, just because they wake up one morning and find they can hit the ball 280 yards, they mustn't assume that this automatically entitles them to enter a PGA tournament. This is an earned right, with certain rules and obligations.

The National Basketball Association has a similar mandatory program for all of its rookies. Unfortunately, tennis has nothing comparable. If you play well, you're welcomed into the game with open arms without any initiation.

With the rarest of exceptions, pro tennis players have no sense of the history of the game that they're playing. They only want to know about what they're doing today, where they're going tomorrow, who's taking them there, and who'll carry their bags and arrange court time for them. And where the nearest bank is. A few players do, however, genuinely care about their sport and its links to the past. They try to work for its continued success. Chris Evert is one of those players. She appreciates tennis history, understands her role as a pivotal person in the game, and does all she can to promote the sport she loves. Often she goes out of her way to sit down and talk to the old-timers, as well as to the youngsters playing the game. She's disturbed by the lack of knowledge about the evolution of women's tennis that she sees among her fellow players.

Once Evert was waiting in the players' lounge before going out to play in the finals of a tournament. Her opponent was there with her. Evert looked up at a photo

of Maureen Connolly, a player who at 16 was the youngest ever to win the U.S. Singles title, and two years later
in 1953 was the first woman to win the Grand Slam.
Chris remarked to her opponent that she hoped one day
to be as good as Little Mo.

The woman stared blankly at the photo. She had no
idea who Evert was talking about. She had never heard
of Connolly and hadn't the faintest idea of her connec-
tion to tennis. This ignorance upset and angered Chris.

Bjorn Borg, a player who made millions of dollars
from tennis, is just the opposite of Evert. In 1987 he
refused to fly from his summer home in Sweden to
Newport, Rhode Island, to attend his induction into the
International Tennis Hall of Fame.

I'd like to see players, retired and active, demonstrate
more willingness to help tennis on a grass roots level.
This means helping out at coaching clinics, meeting
with junior players and critiquing their game, and offering pointers where needed. Although this doesn't sound
like much, it can certainly make a big impact. If only
players would give of themselves once or twice a year,
their "star quality" could mean an awful lot to a struggling tennis program or could be just what's needed to
keep a group of kids interested in continuing to play
tennis instead of wandering off to baseball or some
other sport.

One of my greatest personal pleasures in tennis is to
serve as master of ceremonies at the International Tennis Hall of Fame gala dinner held the last Friday night
during the two weeks of the U.S. Open. Here I get to
chat and renew old ties with the Hall of Famers who
come to the dinner. Later on, it's my privilege to intro-
duce them to the audience. A few of the many wonderful athletes who have been toasted at this annual event
are Alice Marble (U.S. Singles 1936, 1938–1940; Wim-

bledon Singles 1939), Don Budge (U.S. Singles and Wimbledon Singles 1937; Grand Slam 1938), Jack Kramer (U.S. Singles 1946–1947; Wimbledon Singles 1947), and Fred Perry (U.S. Singles 1933–1934, 1936; Wimbledon Singles 1933, 1935–1936). It's a rare treat to talk with these greats of tennis, reliving memories, and exchanging ideas with each of them.

I wish that today's players could spend some time in the company of our living tennis legends. If they were exposed to these impressive personalities, they might appreciate the inherent dignity and graciousness of those who struggled long and hard for personal bests and garnered a few medals of their own along the way.

Most of today's players seem to exist in a vacuum. They have no traditions, no heroes or heroines, no grasp of the history of the game they play. They miss out on the social and historical aspect of tennis, and that is really a shame.

10
Money and
Other Matters

I n late 1955 I joined Jack Kramer's pro tour, leaving the amateur circuit ranked number 1 in the world. I had won 19 of the 23 tournaments I played in that year and was looking forward to finally making some money at tennis. I was also eagerly anticipating going up against the great Richard "Pancho" Gonzales, a player I would place now as one of the all-time Top 10 players in the history of tennis.

My first time out on the tour, I played for 14 straight months and traveled all over the world. In one five-month stretch in North America, Pancho and I played each other 101 times. Pancho served so well and held his service so easily most of the time that I had a struggle on my hands whenever we played. Although I had better groundstrokes than he, even if I practiced my serves for the rest of my life, I'd never come close to being able to serve as well as Pancho. He ended up beating me 74 times out of the 101 matches that we played. The winner of the U.S. National Championships at Forest Hills when he was 20 and again a year later in 1949, Gonzales quickly abandoned the amateur ranks and went on Jack Kramer's pro tour shortly after his second Forest Hills victory.

Pancho had what I consider to be the perfect build for a tennis player. He stood about 6'2", weighed around 180 pounds, and moved extremely well for a guy that size, covering the court with a quickness that would leave me exasperated. In today's game, Yannick Noah of France is the one player who comes closest to Pancho's physical stature and athleticism.

But Pancho's greatest asset was his cannonball serve, which moved at least 110 miles per hour. Although his groundstrokes weren't the best, they were certainly good. Just ask Charlie Pasarell, who engaged Pancho in a five-hour, 12-minute match that lasted a Wimbledon-record 112 games. Even at the age of 41, Gonzales hated to lose and beat the younger Pasarell 22–24, 1–6, 16–14, 6–3, 11–9.

I grossed $125,000 during that first 14-month tour. Since the Kramer players couldn't play in any of the major tournaments because of our pro status, we'd set up anywhere in the world that people would pay to see us play. This meant one-night stands on the five continents, playing tennis on a portable court we'd lug around with us when necessary. We'd play in gymnasiums, open-air markets, and small arenas from Paris to Pocatello. This was a great time in my life. Nobody forced me to do what I was doing, and I loved everything about it.

I left Jack Kramer's pro tour in 1963, basically because I had lost the eagerness to pay the price needed to keep in top shape. I was 33 years old, I had a family, and there just wasn't much money to be made in pro tennis

at that time. All this would start to change five years
later. Total prize money in 1968, the first year of Open
Tennis when the pros could finally play in the same
tournaments as amateurs, was estimated at $350,000.
For winning Wimbledon that year, Rod Laver received
the princely sum of £2,000 (about $5,000). By 1987,
worldwide tournament tennis purses had almost surpassed $35 million, with the U.S. Open giving record-
setting $250,000 checks to the winner of the mens' and
womens' singles championships.

I have to chuckle when I hear pro players complain
that the life they've cut out for themselves is difficult.
Jimmy Connors has earned well over $7 million in prize
money alone from playing tennis in a successful career
that dates back to the early 1970s. He's won two Wimbledon titles, six other Grand Slam championships, and
has 105 tournament victories to his credit, the men's
record.

Yet Jimbo moans that the tournament-playing schedule he keeps often has him leapfrogging from the Far
East to South America, on to Europe, then back home
again in successive weeks without a chance for any rest
and recuperation. He gets tired from the globe hopping
and says that tennis players, more than any other pro
athletes, are defying the laws of nature when they run
around like this.

After playing tennis most of his 35 years, Jimbo now
admits that he would never want either of his two children to follow in his footsteps, because the life of a
tennis player is not a "natural life for anyone." That
may be, but I've yet to hear of any tennis official roam-
ing around out there who's got a gun to Jimmy's head
forcing him or any other pro player to pack his bags
every week and march out to the airport with his
rackets.

The Men's Tennis Council (MTC), which administers and operates men's professional tennis out of its New York and Paris offices, mandates that the top 100 singles players participate in a minimum of 14 tournaments each year. Tournament tennis is classified and made up of the four Grand Slam events (Australian Open, French Open, Wimbledon, and U.S. Open), each of which lasts two weeks, and 34 Nabisco Super Series Grand Prix Series events, which last a week or less. Grand Slam and Super Series events each have minimum prize purses of $340,000 going all the way up to and exceeding $1 million. These events are understandably popular with all of the players, but only the Top 10 players (according to their computer ranking from the previous season) are allowed to select their 14 tournaments from only the Grand Slam and Super Series list.

Singles players with world rankings from 11 through 25 have to play in 14 tournaments as well, but two of these have to be from the Regular Series tournament list. The Regular Series events are tournaments that have a ceiling on purses at $330,000, with some tournaments offering as "little" as $123,400 in total prizes. Players ranked 26–75 can select eleven Grand Slam or Super Series events and three Regular Series tournaments, while those ranked 76–100 can select ten Grand Slam or Super Series events and four Regular Series tournaments.

The top 100 players can choose where and when they want to play, as long as they agree to play the minimum of 14 scheduled tournaments and the Nabisco Masters and WCT Finals if they qualify. By mid-September prior to the new calendar year, they must submit in writing to the MTC the list of tournaments that they'll commit to play in the following year. A player who wanted could plan a season consisting solely of these 14 tournaments. Of course, many choose to play in more because the lure of the financial reward is so powerful.

Still, the grumbling that goes on from the players, upset that they have to expend all that energy and skill for such a measly amount of money, is incredible. If the top players had their way, playing in lucrative exhibitions that promoters like to stage as often as possible, a few Grand Slam or big-money Super Series events, possibly Davis Cup or Federation Cup play, would be all that they'd ever choose to participate in.

There's a lot of easy money to be made in exhibitions. By capitalizing on their personal athletic stature built up through a successful tournament career that includes Grand Slam victories, top players can lure thousands of tennis fans to buy tickets to see them perform.

How the players actually perform in an exhibition is another matter altogether. Not Wimbledon by any stretch of the imagination, these matches are purely entertainment rather than sport. Their outcome has absolutely no bearing on a player's computer ranking or world standing. Think of them as a spring-training exhibition baseball game where the ballplayers will go hard for a little while, working only on particular aspects of their game. The baseball players and the fans who come to these Grapefruit League games know that they're not going to be stellar performances of the kind they'd expect in October at World Series time.

Tennis fans should clearly understand that in a two-player exhibition, both players may get the same amount of money for appearing ($75,000 and upward), and it seldom matters to either of them who wins and who loses. In their minds, it's money that counts, and that they've already won. Of course, all exhibition matches are hyped in the local press as if they were going to be a "big event," but that's only because the

TENTATIVE PROVISIONAL 1988 NABISCO GRAND PRIX CALENDAR AS OF JANUARY 6, 1987

WEEK BEGIN.	GRAND SLAM/ SUPER SERIES, ETC.	DRAW	***PLAYER COMPENSATION	REGULAR OPEN SERIES	DRAW	PLAYER COMPENSATION
DEC 28				*Adelaide	(32)	123,400
				*Wellington	(32)	145,000
JAN 4				*Aukland	(32)	123,400
				*Sydney NSW	(32)	123,400
11	Australian Open (5)	(128)	1,054,984			
18	Australian Open					
25				*Guaruja	(32)	130,000
FEB 1	(Davis Cup—1st Round)					
8	Rotterdam	(32)	442,500	Lyon	(32)	270,000
15	Memphis (5)	(48)	415,000			
	Milan (5)	(32)	490,000			
22	Philadelphia (5)	(48)	* 602,500	Metz	(32)	123,400
29	Indian Wells (5)	(56)	702,500			
	(European Cup)					
MAR 7	Orlando	(32)	415,000			
14	Key Biscayne	(128)	1,025,000			
21	Key Biscayne					
28	WCT Finals	(8)	680,000			
APR 4	(Davis Cup—2nd Round)					
11	Tokyo (Suntory)	(56)	* 617,500	Nice	(32)	145,000
18	Monte Carlo (5)	(48)	492,500	Madrid	(32)	123,400
25	Hamburg (5)	(56)	592,500	Seoul	(32)	123,400
				Charleston	(32)	220,000

WEEK BEGIN.	GRAND SLAM/ SUPER SERIES, ETC.	DRAW	***PLAYER COMPENSATION	REGULAR OPEN SERIES	DRAW	PLAYER COMPENSATION
MAY 2	New York—TOC (5)	(64)	677,500	Munich	(48)	195,000
9	Rome (5)	(64)	787,500	*Florence	(32)	123,400
16	(World Team Cup)	(128)	TBA			
23	French Open (5)					
30	French Open					
JUN 6				*Queens	(64)	320,000
				*Bologna	(32)	123,400
13				*Bristol	(48)	123,400
				*Athens	(32)	123,400
20	Wimbledon (5)	(128)	TBA			
27	Wimbledon					
JULY 4	Boston	(56)	415,000	Newport	(32)	145,000
				Gstaad (5)	(32)	245,000
11				Bastad (5)	(48)	245,000
				Stuttgart	(48)	305,000
				Schenectady	(32)	123,400
18	Washington (Davis Cup—3rd Round)	(56)	415,000	Hilversum (5)	(32)	170,000
25	Stratton Mountain	(64)	592,500	Bordeaux	(32)	245,000
AUG 1	Indianapol s	(56)	415,000	Kitzbuhel (5)	(64)	270,000
8	Toronto	(56)	*602,500	St. Vincent	(32)	123,400
				Prague	(32)	170,000
15	Cincinnati	(64)	602,500	Livingston	(32)	123,400
22				*Rye Brook	(32)	123,400
29	U.S. Open (5)	(128)	TBA			

WEEK BEGIN.	GRAND SLAM/ SUPER SERIES, ETC.	DRAW	***PLAYER COMPENSATION	REGULAR OPEN SERIES	DRAW	PLAYER COMPENSATION
SEPT 5	U.S. Open					
12	Barcelona (5)	(56)	490,000			
19	Los Angeles	(32)	415,000	Geneva	(32)	220,000
				*Bari	(32)	123,400
				Palermo	(32)	123,400
26	San Francisco	(32)	415,000			
OCT 3	Scottsdale	(32)	415,000	Brisbane	(32)	195,000
				Basle (5)	(32)	270,000
10	Sydney Indoor (5)	(32)	490,000	Tel Aviv	(32)	125,000
				Toulouse	(32)	245,000
				Vienna (5)	(32)	145,000
17	Tokyo (Seiko)	(32)	617,500			
24	Paris (5)	(32)	1,077,500			
31	Stockholm (5)	(56)	642,500	Sao Paulo	(32)	130,000
NOV 7	London (5)	(32)	452,500	Frankfurt	(32)	170,000
				Buenos Aires	(32)	123,400
14	**Johannesburg (5)	(32)	590,000			
	Detroit	(32)	415,000			
21	Brussels	(32)	490,000	Itaparica	(32)	516,000
28	Nabisco Masters	(8)	TBA			
DEC 5	Nabisco Masters Doubles	(8)	277,500			
12	(Davis Cup—Finals)					

GRAND SLAM/SUPER

Player Compensation	On-Site Distribution
277,500	200,000
415,000	297,500
442,500	325,000
452,500	335,000
490,000	372,500
492,500	375,000
590,000	297,500
592,500	400,000
* 602,500	410,000
602,500	485,000
* 617,500	425,000
617,500	500,000
642,500	450,000
677,500	485,000
680,000	500,000
702,500	510,000
787,500	595,000
1,025,000	745,000
1,054,984	699,984
1,077,500	810,000

REGULAR/OPEN WEEK

Player Compensation	On-Site Distribution
123,400	93,400
125,000	95,000
130,000	100,000
145,000	115,000
155,000	125,000
170,000	140,000
195,000	165,000
220,000	190,000
245,000	215,000
255,000	225,000
270,000	240,000
305,000	275,000
320,000	290,000
516,000	398,500

* Open Week Series Tournaments (Non-Designated)
** $297,500 On-Site
$100,000 Travel Allowance:
   $2,700.00—Singles Players
   $1,350.00—Doubles Players Only
*** Does not include amounts offered as player hospitality which are also considered player compensation

CORRECTIONS/CHANGES SINCE DEC. 31 CALENDAR:

Sao Paulo—Player compensation increase
Hong Kong—Cancelled
Stratton Mt.—Correction to player compensation
Tokyo Seiko—Correction to player compensation
Toulouse—Correction to player compensation
Player compensation/on-site figures amended

Men's International Professional Tennis Council

4th Floor 437 Madison Avenue   Stade Roland Garros
New York, NY 10022   2 Avenue Gordon Bennett
(212) 838-8450 Telex 968145   75016 Paris France
Telecopier (212) 759-9528   33-1-4743-1600 Telex 612051
Cable GRANDPRIX NEWYORK   Telecopier 33-1-4651-0241

players' respective agents (often both exhibition players have the same one, making for a very cozy deal) stand to gain financially from attendance and concession sales.

What you would hope to see in a good exhibition is a display of skills: two world-class players performing nicely. You'll often see some humor as well. You'll get to see players as human beings who can smile and aren't as grim as they are in tournament play, where their reputations, ranking, and winner's check are all on the line. Exhibition players might hit the ball behind their backs, but don't expect to see them dive for too many out-of-reach shots. This isn't to say that you won't see some terrific tennis. Since the players are relaxed and under no real pressure on any given point, they're apt to make more good shots. You'll see angle volleys, drop volleys, and a lot of fancy stuff that they normally wouldn't think of trying under tournament conditions.

I have no gripes whatsoever with players who go to play in exhibitions. It shows that they're smart enough to take advantage of their names and reputations. My complaint with exhibitions comes when they're purposely scheduled to conflict with already scheduled tournament tennis. Luring top players away from the tour, having them bypass these big tournaments to go and hit tennis balls in a meaningless exhibition, damages the professional tour and ultimately tennis the sport.

When tennis as sport gives way to tennis as mere entertainment, the game gets set back a few years. According to Gladys Heldman, writing in *World Tennis* magazine, a classic case of this occurred several years ago when Donald Dell of ProServ got all the big names to play in the Suntory Cup, an exhibition he had set up in Japan. With money already in their bank accounts, the players rushed over to Japan, in the meantime making themselves unavailable for a tournament scheduled in Houston that was counting on their appearance to make it a success. In this instance, Dell, Suntory, and the players each benefited to the detriment of the Houston tournament in particular and the pro tour in general.

"I'm constantly battling with the pros because they're always complaining to me that they don't have enough time to practice for the big matches," says Marshall Happer III, administrator of the MTC. "But you can be sure that if the player's agent calls to say he's got an exhibition lined up in Paris for the next day, that same player who just told me that he didn't have time for practice would be off to the airport in a minute, play in the exhibition, and be home in time for dinner the following day."

The scenario seems to be the same lately: once a player finally makes it to the top of the heap, the newly arrived player tries to forget about the tennis system that nurtured him or her along the way. Now this player wants to start dictating the terms.

The MTC has included relatively low-paying tournaments on the yearly schedule for one very good reason. It's in the best interests of everyone concerned to bring the sport of tennis to as many places, to as many parts of the world, and to as many people as possible. Granted, some tournaments may not offer bundles of money, but the mere presence of top players at these little tournaments guarantees a certain pizzazz and helps fill the stadium. This in turn sparks interest in the people who come to the matches to play tennis, to buy equipment, and to return the following year to watch the matches. If they're lucky, tournament organizers might even be able to snag a sponsor who'll spring for

TV coverage, thereby affording even more exposure for their tournament. Needless to say, this kind of participation on a local level helps the game of tennis enormously on a national level.

If the MTC didn't require top players to play in some of these small tournaments, then you could be sure that they'd run off at the first chance to play in the many lucrative exhibitions staged by their agents. Of course, they'd still come to the remaining big-money tournaments, but I'll bet you the winner's prize at the U.S. Open they'd make a point of boycotting any tournament that didn't meet their financial standards. If players were allowed to decide the number of tournaments they wanted to play in or to randomly pick and choose these events—and certain agents would love to see this happen—the tennis tour would be dead within a decade.

Tennis players need to be raised properly by parents who teach them about loyalty and appreciation. With these values the players will be grateful for the tennis structure that brought them along with junior and satellite programs and helped keep them on their feet when they had little money. They'll understand that tennis needs their continued support once they finally make a name for themselves, and that being a professional means more than just playing the game and depositing a paycheck. In too many instances, tennis players on the tour are a greedy bunch. So many are selfish and spoiled, taking all they can, while giving so little in return. They're not at all concerned about killing the golden goose, but only in finding ways to make it produce even more.

Tennis is different from other professional sports in that it's always been an individual sport with no links to a specific city or region, and it doesn't get support on that level. There have been people who have tried to change this however. In 1974, World Team Tennis (WTT) was launched in an effort to buck the trend and capitalize on the love affair Americans have for team sports. Men and women made up the rosters of the 16 original teams in the U.S. and competed together for the first time. Among the top players in the new league were Chris Evert, Evonne Goolagong, John Newcombe, and Fred Stolle. However, high player salaries and half-filled arenas finally convinced the team owners that the team concept wasn't working. They closed up shop after the 1978 season.

Team tennis in not yet dead in this country, but is still surviving away from the glitter of the big cities. Billie Jean King, whose husband Larry King was an original founder of WTT, is now the driving force behind the Domino's Team Tennis circuit, a relatively new six-team league that operates without big-name players and plays in smaller U.S. cities during the summer. While I have my doubts that team tennis can ever work in a big way in this country because of the underlying individual nature of the sport and the inflated salaries that marquee value players would command, King firmly believes that the team tennis concept works because in addition to sponsoring the pro league, Domino's Pizza also sponsors grass roots age-group competition for children right up through adults aged 60 and over. "The bottom line is that we need more tennis in this country," King said. "People are looking for opportunities to play as well as to watch top-flight competition, and Domino's is bringing the tennis loving public what it wants."

While only time will tell if King is successful marketing and promoting her new league, self-promotion and a bit of good public relations is also something that professional tennis players need if they want to keep their sport going at its current high level of public acceptance.

What do most of the top men players do to help their sport? Frankly, very little. They complain about being tired from all the airplane travel they have to do, even when they take the Concorde. If players weren't so avaricious, they would demand that their managers change their schedule so they wouldn't have to be in Tokyo one week in a tournament, Buenos Aires the next for an exhibition, and Paris the following week to fulfill an endorsement commitment. But since money is the motivator, they race through time zones as often as they change their socks, griping all the way. They deserve sympathy from no one and should get none on this score. Top players have control over 95 percent of what they do, of when and where they play. Ivan Lendl was quoted as having said, "Tennis has no off season." My response: If that's the case, then why not create your own?

In tennis, it's no longer a question of whether top players will earn enough money to support their families. The question really is how much, if any, they are willing to pass up. I know of some traveling salespeople who are on the road at least two-thirds of the year. That's how they can make a decent living. But I promise you, it's nothing like the living the top pros make.

Many players are so hooked on the success that they get from the game that they become addicted to the adulation of their fans. Then there's an additional rush they get from the tremendous sums of money that they earn. What too many of these players fail to realize, however, is that they can't have everything. If they're playing tennis most of the year, then they can't expect to get proper rest. Often, they won't have time for friends or a complete family life. To integrate these normal human relationships into their schedules, they'd have to get off the tour periodically and make time for them. But missing a tournament or exhibition would also mean making less money. Ah, there's the rub!

Essentially, tennis players are motivated by ambition for personal success and, in some cases, greed. They have a burning desire to get a foothold on the ladder and stay on top of the good life for as long as they can. Like the hard-driven salespeople, they must pay a stiff price for this type of maneuvering. And although many of the players complain about the sacrifice they have to make, most do little to change when it's so obviously within their power to do so.

The top players make so much money and they play so often that I have to wonder whether they ever have a chance to enjoy the wealth and status they have achieved. And don't think for a minute that the cold cash they pick up for winning tournaments is all that they get. As a matter of fact, their winner's checks are barely the tip of the Big Green Iceberg that floats around the tennis tour.

By any world standards, $1.9 million a year (Ivan Lendl and Martina Navratilova each earned this much in 1986 for tournament play) is a pretty decent annual wage. Actually, what's not included in this listing is money earned from paid endorsements from such game-related sources as racket manufacturers, shoe companies, and apparel makers. Depending on the world ranking of the player and the aggressiveness of his or her agent, this extra booty could swell to an additional $1 to $5 million annually. Again, a pretty decent annual wage.

When you read the sports pages with their reports about deals and endorsements, it's often easy to confuse them with the business pages. After a while, you have to start asking yourself, "Are these players carrying around tennis rackets or attaché cases?"

A quick look at a player's shirt will give you a good idea of who's best at feathering the nest with endorsement deals. Not yet as blatant as Tour de France bicycle racers, who sell promotional space on every available part of their jerseys, tennis players are certainly catching up quickly.

Soon after 18-year-old Steffi Graf led her West German squad to its first-ever victory over Chris Evert and her teammates in Federation Cup competition in 1987, *Advertising Age* reported that Graf signed an endorsement contract with a West German fruit juice company for $550,000. This "modest" amount allows the company to use her photos in their advertisements.

Big contract for a little kid? Hardly. According to the *Advertising Age* report, this check gets deposited right into the pile of endorsement cash already earning interest from Adidas USA ($500,000 for wearing their tennis clothing and sneakers), Opel cars ($670,000 for newspaper and magazine ads), Hatex ($390,000 for wearing their clothing), and Jade ($390,000 for endorsing their cosmetic line). Every time she appears at a tennis exhibition, Graf pulls down another $50,000 at least.

Graf does have some limits on what she will do to enhance her renown. She didn't seriously consider posing au naturel for *Penthouse* and had no qualms about turning down the reported $240,000 inducement.

For all the cash Graf is raking in, fellow countryman Boris "Boom Boom" Becker tops her estimated $3.3 million yearly haul, according to *Advertising Age* by taking home a reported $4.8 million for his off-court hustle. All of this for a player that 75 percent of Germans polled found to be "ill-tempered, moody, and pompous."

Many pro players, male and female, have no idea of what a good life they have. That's because they've been pampered and spoiled since they first showed inklings of talent. Pushed by parents who dreamed of the money a pro life would offer their kids (and them), driven by coaches who believed only in winning (and who hoped to become the personal coach of a winner), and regularly wined, dined, cornered, and 10–25 percented by avaricious agents who see only dollar signs, it's not really surprising that most of today's players are not a well-rounded, affable lot. "Me first" is their credo, and everybody else had better look out or risk getting trampled. Or ignored.

11
The Dark Side: Guarantees and Tanking

I n addition to endorsements, exhibitions, and tournament winnings, there's another way for a player to add to his or her gravy train. That comes from sticking out a hand and asking a tournament promoter for a guarantee.

Plainly and simply, a guarantee is appearance money. A bribe. It's an illegal inducement by a tournament promoter to get a player to commit to play in a particular tournament. Sometimes the bribe is given in the form of cold cash; other times it's a drastic reduction on or outright gift of an expensive car. Although I certainly can't prove it, it's rumored around the circuit that guarantees are regularly paid to some of the top players and that they've become a standard way for promoters to do business with players (or player's agents) in today's game.

In the days before open tennis, some "shamateur" players would be paid by tournament promoters to

show up and help increase the gate. Payment was sometimes in the form of paying off a wager. "I'll bet you
can't jump over that can of tennis balls," the promoter
would say to the player. After the player easily stepped
over the can, he'd get a sum of money for his efforts.
After a while, this subterfuge was dispensed with altogether, and payments were made outright.

Just as in the old days, when shamateur players
would meet with tournament directors to settle up on
their cut for deigning to show up for a match, promoters are once again saying, "Hey, if I can get the number
1 ranked player in the world to come to my tournament,
I'll draw more people through the turnstiles, have a better chance to get more sponsorship money, and have a
better chance for television money. So I give him
$100,000 for showing up; what's the big deal? He helps
me, and I help him. If he wins the tournament, that's
even more money for him."

A possible drawback to this scheme is that once the
promoter has used up the under-the-table appearance
money and paid off the top players, he or she no longer
has any money left for some other top pro who might
show up with open hands. The promoter not only loses
this player but also the opportunity for the best possible
competitive tournament.

No matter what anyone else might say, watching the
number 1 player in the world waltz through to the finals
by knocking off number 20 or number 40 in the world
really doesn't make for the most inspiring tennis. Only
when the top players go at it head to head, when there's
some parity in the competitive level, will tennis fans see
truly inspiring tennis.

If the huge sums of money now set aside for appearance guarantees were put back into the pot of available
prize money and then all the top players actually came

to play, each one starting out with empty pockets in round 1, tennis fans would truly see more great tennis every time they went to a match. The stars of the game would have to prove on the court that they are in fact the stars and not just paid performers trundled in by a promoter for their marquee value.

Unfortunately, when it comes to accepting these bribes, some tennis players seem to listen to their unscrupulous advisors. Their attitude, based on lack of honor and enormous greed, soon becomes "no pay, no play." In effect, they say, "If it weren't for me, the tournament wouldn't be drawing all the people that it does. I deserve the money, so give it to me."

This faulty reasoning goes against the whole concept of open tennis, which came into being 20 years ago to stop under-the-table payments, make them illegal, and to let players compete for prize money based only on merit. Tennis players compete in order to pit their skills against one another, to try to best an opponent and go on to the next round.

The whole rationale behind the pro game is the better someone plays, the more money he or she makes. When players no longer have to win in order to make money, they're apt to lose all incentive for living up to their athletic code of honor to give the best performance they're capable of.

Some players will try to convince you that they give their all in a tournament even though they've been paid handsomely in advance just for showing up. "I won't get guarantees in the future if I don't win, so I always play my best so I won't lose," they'll say.

I don't believe them for a minute. If a player doesn't have to fight as hard as he or she can to earn the money, then that player just won't. In the end, as this will to win slowly diminishes, the credibility, the "cleanliness" of tennis as a sport starts to come into question. And the day that the public views tennis as some form of pro wrestling is the beginning of the end for professional tennis.

The MTC has done its best to crack down on guarantees, but with only a five-person supervisory staff and the entire world as its territory, the job is difficult, if not virtually impossible.

In one rare instance, Guillermo Vilas of Argentina was fired for taking money to appear in a Grand Prix tournament in Rotterdam, a tournament he ended up losing. Vilas was fined $20,000—if Vilas really did take the appearance money, then he still made $40,000 on the deal, but no one at the MTC talks about that—and suspended from the tour. Dutch tournament organizers were also fined $10,000 for their part in the matter.

Top players have tremendous star magnetism, like that of movie stars or pop musicians. To capitalize on this, they'll often try to increase their earning potential by playing in exhibitions right before and after Grand Prix tournaments. "We're not against this at all," says Happer. "Nor do we see anything wrong with a top player trying to maximize his earnings by doing store appearances or TV work while he's in town for a tournament. We look at this as being incidental to his main reason for being in a city, which is to play tournament tennis. What we [MTC] construe to be wrong is if a player tells a tournament director that he won't come to play in his tournament unless store appearances or endorsements are made available where he can make an outrageous fee. Then this becomes another matter altogether."

This "matter" Happer speaks about has also become a gray area in professional tennis. Since international corporations now regularly make it a practice to sign top players to endorsement contracts worth hundreds of thousands of dollars, the unsolvable question for the MTC has become whether the player's endorsement contract was the bait to get the player to compete in a tournament that has close links with the corporate sponsor. Or was the endorsement contract actually given after the player had already agreed to play in the tournament? In such a chicken-or-egg instance, it's proving difficult to set policy. Many situations have recently developed in these gray areas and unfortunately may never be cleared up.

In the end, the question of guarantees has to come down to personal ethics and how a particular player was raised. If pro players can't see that they're hurting the sport by accepting guarantees, then something surely has gone awry. Players can make all the money they want in tennis, but by continuing to take it under the table, they're steadily chipping away at the moral foundation of the game. In a matter of years, if these abuses aren't shored up, the game will all come tumbling down around them and the stars of tomorrow.

Along with the proliferation of guarantees, in recent years there's been an increase in the instances of players who "tank," or intentionally give up the match for one reason or another. Someone who tanks a match will play with considerably less than 100 percent intensity because he or she "couldn't get into the game" or "just didn't feel like playing" that particular day. The player chooses to lose 6–0 or 6–1 in the final set, pick up the check, and run off to the next tournament with the spectators' boos still ringing in his or her ears.

Pro players are obligated to the ticket buyers as well as to themselves to give their best effort every time they step on the court. This doesn't mean that a spectator is necessarily going to see a player in top form, or that the

Tim Mayotte is a mentally and physically tough competitor from New England—
a professional in the truest sense of the word. Whenever he takes to the court you
know that you'll see him give his all for the entire match.

PHOTO COURTESY OF AP/WORLDWIDE PHOTOS

player will even win the match. But you do want to be able to walk away after the match saying, "Boy, that guy sure gave everything that he had!"

Giving their best is all you can ask of players. Unfortunately you don't get this all of the time from today's pros. I've seen too many 6–0 or 6–1 scores in the last set, and it's starting to bother me because it shows that the losing player was most likely dogging it and just going through the motions.

After a certain point in a match, some players think that they can't win, so they basically give up. Some will later claim they were "dizzy" or felt a "little sick." Other times, when players see that it will take too much effort to win, they might just say "What the heck? I'll get him next time" and then go into the tank.

When tanking goes on, the players don't make it obvious by just standing there and letting balls go by. It's a lot more subtle than that. I can often tell that a player isn't trying simply by the way the player acts, by his or her posture on the court. I can see it in the player's eyes and expression.

The increase in tanking is probably tied up with the enormous sums of money now made available for losing. Losers, even in the early rounds of some tournaments, stand to make thousands of dollars. And if they can make this much without playing well, when they find themselves behind in a match, many succumb to the temptation by pulling back and losing, rather than trying their best to win. They quit!

Tanking isn't just endemic to tennis. I've seen it on the pro golf tour when a player shoots a 78 in the opening round, and a "WD" is posted after his name in the standings. WD stands for "withdrew." The golfer will justify dropping out as a way to avoid burdening the tournament or the other players with his or her presence. But the bottom line is that the player just didn't want to have to play anymore after falling so far behind in the standings, and having no realistic chance of winning.

As an athlete, I've always believed that if you enter a tournament, barring an injury, you have a firm obligation to finish that tournament at full throttle, no matter how poorly you may be playing. Byron Nelson, one of the all-time great golfers, once told me that some of the best rounds of golf he ever had came when he opened with a 75 or 76 and had a few double bogeys. Although Nelson had a strong urge to throw his clubs in the car and take off, he ground it out in the next rounds and forced himself to play well.

"If I didn't improve in those rounds, I didn't earn a paycheck," said Nelson, "and my bills didn't get paid."

I seldom see this determination to come from behind as much in tennis. A few years ago when I was at a tournament in Japan, I saw two top pros play in a semifinal. After a close first set, the loser basically lost his desire to go on and quit in the second set, losing 6–1. In the finals, the winner from the night before played a great opening set against another top pro. Although he lost 7–5, it was a thrilling duel that had the normally staid Japanese fans cheering wildly. Surprisingly, instead of coming back on the court all fired up and ready to win the second set, this so-called "pro" proceeded to go into the tank, losing without much of a fight. He took his hefty runner-up check and his expensive watch, and left for the airport. In essence, he'd played one hard set. Once he saw that he was going to have a dogfight on his hands in order to win the title, he found it easier to give up.

Officially, according to the MTC guidelines, a Grand Prix supervisor must be present at the court and then take appropriate action to have a player penalized for tanking. However, tanking is difficult to prove conclusively. Some players could just be frustrated at not making their shots and appear not to be trying. Which official is going to make a call on the reason why someone's play has suddenly become flat? Try running that one by John McEnroe.

At the U.S. Open doubles finals in 1985, Americans Ken Flach and Robert Seguso split their first two sets with Frenchmen Yannick Noah and Henri Leconte. After one spirited exchange at the net, in which Leconte's shot hit the tape, then bounced by Flach's ear and landed out over the baseline, Noah and Leconte became upset because they felt that the ball had nicked Flach's long hair before going out. They wanted Flach to admit to this, but Flach remained mute on the subject, with Noah and Leconte losing the point.

After much debate with the chair umpire, the crowd began hooting and hollering. The Frenchmen's protest was ignored, and play was ordered continued, with the point staying with the Americans. It had been set point in the tie break for the French team. Leconte and Noah then lost another set point and eventually the third set. They didn't win another game. Tanking? Only Leconte and Noah know.

Persistence is a much overlooked quality in sports, and it's especially absent in most tankers. If you have this mental strength, however, it's often enough to demoralize an opponent with much more physical talent. If you're a tenacious player and can keep hammering away, not giving up even when things look bleakest, it's amazing what can happen.

In 1984 and 1985 Vic Seixas and I teamed up to play doubles at Wimbledon. In a 1954 quarterfinal round match, we were down 4–6, 14–16 and had lost the first four games of the third set. It looked as if we were heading for the showers. At this time our opponents started getting cute for the gallery and began missing routine shots. In the meantime, we kept plugging away, finally breaking enough serves to come back to win the last three sets and the match. Our opponents had become overconfident, and it ended up costing them the match.

Pride in my athletic skills has always stayed with me, even when I was getting beaten pretty soundly. In an epic Davis Cup Challenge Round match against Lew Hoad in Melbourne in 1953, I lost the first two sets 11–13 and 3–6. I refused to give in and fought back to win the third and fourth sets. I finally lost 7–5 in the fifth, but when I went to the net to shake Hoadie's hand, even though I was disappointed, I knew deep inside that I'd done all that I could possibly do to win. When I was down 2–0 in sets, I never once let myself think that I was out of the match. I told myself that I had to win the next three straight sets, and I systematically started my comeback.

When you can get yourself to think and feel that way, you do occasionally win three straight. And when you don't win, as I didn't against Hoad that day, at least you can tell yourself that you gave it your best shot, you did all that you could to win even when the odds were stacked against you. Disappointed though you may be, when you play tennis with this positive attitude, you're able to walk off the court with your head held high, and promising yourself that you will come back and win the next time.

12
The Administrators
of the Pro Game:
Constant Evolution

At 20 years old, Open tennis is relatively young compared to other professional sports. Along with the tremendous influx of money into the game in the past two decades has come the increasing presence and influence of sports agents. Agents first got in the front door of professional tennis on day 1 and essentially took over the house. This was allowed to happen because tennis had been traditionally run by well-intentioned volunteers who gave what time they could to running a tournament after they first put in time at their primary jobs. It was certainly not unheard of, but definitely was uncommon, to have paid, full-time employees who worked day to day at business related to tennis tournaments. That's why, when sports agents first approached various tournament committees and pointed out how they could arrange for sponsorship and television coverage, as well as perform all the other duties now handled by volunteer committees (often not too well), many tournaments gave them carte blanche to do just that.

In my opinion, two agents in particular, Donald Dell—a Washington, D.C., lawyer and one of the founders of ProServ, a successful sports marketing group—and Mark McCormack—the founder and director of International Management Group (IMG) out of Cleveland, the first of the great sports marketers in America—have developed an unhealthy stranglehold on tennis. These two men are presently shaking the very foundation of the professional game with their international deal cutting.

Donald Dell's estimated $25 million–plus a year ProServ roots are sunk deeply in tennis. Dell was formerly a highly ranked amateur player and later captained the Davis Cup team (1968–1969). By 1970, just six years out of law school, he became the aggressive attorney/ agent/business representative for Arthur Ashe, Stan Smith, Bob Lutz, and Charlie Pasarell, the leading players of the day. With these stars as a solid nucleus, Dell landed endorsement and licensing deals for his clients. In 1972 he helped put together and then legally represented the Association of Tennis Professionals (ATP), the men's union. Dell also helped form the original Grand Prix circuit, then branched out to get TV rights for tournaments. He also began staging lucrative exhibitions around the world for his clients and started representing corporate tournament sponsors. In a matter of a few years, ProServ offices were sprouting in the capitals of major countries worldwide to help Dell manage his burgeoning empire.

In 1960 Mark McCormack got started in the sports business in similar fashion by first handling the business affairs of golfer Arnold Palmer. Although Palmer was a top player, he was earning only $60,000 a year, a sum McCormack helped push to $500,000 in just two years through shrewd investing, hype, merchandising, and the marketing of Palmer's name and image to corporate America.

McCormack, 57, streetsmart, savvy, and a tough negotiator, is now a self-made millionaire many times over. His IMG empire now includes 15 offices worldwide, which pull in revenues in the hundreds of millions of dollars. In addition to representing Martina Navratilova and Chris Evert, along with a slew of other players, he also negotiates the TV rights on behalf of the U.S. Open and Wimbledon and advised the Calgary Winter Olympic committee. It's also now being whispered that IMG will start its own professional golf tour by trying to lure the top players away from the PGA Tour. It should be interesting to see what happens in this regard.

Today, Dell and McCormack not only represent many of the top tennis players in contract and endorsement deals, which is what a typical sport agent does. They also organize and promote tennis tournaments, attain and negotiate sponsorship fees, invite select players to participate in their tournaments, give wild card invitations to some of their own struggling clients, and obtain television rights. Dell also personally goes on TV, appearing to be an impartial analyst to viewers unfamiliar with his background.

ProServ and IMG, among the dominant agencies in tennis, offer complete packages that keep tennis players, various Grand Prix and exhibition tournaments, and many corporate sponsors very happy. But this has led to a major conflict with the actual administrators of the pro game, the Men's Tennis Council (MTC). By continuing to go about their business of sponsoring special events that compete with already scheduled tournament tennis, ProServ and IMG add more gray hairs to the head of Marshall Happer, who manages men's pro tennis worldwide through the MTC.

While the U.S. Tennis Association is in charge of governing the amateur game in this country and runs its many tournaments, the MTC schedules tournaments and overseas men's pro tennis. This nine-member body is made up of three player representatives, three tournament reps, and three reps from the national tennis federations. It has now, under Happer's direction, finally started to get tough with anyone who tries to change the course or direction of the pro game.

The actual setup of the Tennis Council, with its three-tiered power base and one administrator, is a fragile democracy at best, especially since it works within a framework based on ethical concepts. The three disparate groups—the players, tournament heads, and federations—form a unique triumvirate not found anywhere else in sport. Together they try to hammer out rulings that show a general concern for the game, even though each group actually represents constituencies that might have a much narrower interest in mind. It's a miracle that the council has been able to work as well as it has.

In a recent development, for example, the players' group wanted more prize money for the major tournaments they play in. While the tournament directors pointed out that the players already received $35 million annually in prize money from the tour, the players contended that they helped raise more than $70 million for the tournaments through their box office appeal. The Council discussed this issue and finally agreed with the players. In 1988 prize money escalated from a $300,000 minimum to $500,000 in each of the Super Series Tournaments.

This kind of close cooperation will enable the Pro

Council, and therefore professional tennis, to move forward in a professional manner. Although the groups within the council may not always be in harmony, discussing the problems will keep the sport from stagnating.

Many have likened Marshall Happer, a former North Carolina trial attorney, to an unofficial tennis "commissioner," a title Happer is quick to disavow. To the dismay of superagents, however, Happer is proving to be a stern watchdog who steers players toward sanctioned events and openly questions and then looks into practices such as guarantees, endorsement contracts, and player appearances.

Not only does Happer disapprove of the multifaceted role agents have taken on to the detriment of the game, but as administrator of the MTC (and with the broader interests of the game in mind), he has aggressively spearheaded lines of attack to curtail the tremendous and far-reaching power of agents by instituting stricter rules, pursuing cases in the courts of law when necessary.

In 1985 the MTC and the tennis agents escalated their years of verbal skirmishing into a full-scale war when a major antitrust lawsuit was filed, surprisingly not by the MTC, but by Volvo, a ProServ client. Volvo, the Swedish automotive company, had formerly been the major sponsor of the men's Grand Prix circuit but had become disgruntled after tournament title sponsorship was given to Nabisco in the early 1980s.

Volvo sued the MTC, claiming that the MTC lacked the sovereign right to govern men's pro tennis. This, of course, was an effort to stop what Volvo saw as the growing power of the MTC and their resulting loss of leverage. The agents, Dell and McCormack, sided with Volvo.

In the summer of 1987, the U.S. District Court threw

out Volvo's suit, dismissing all of the antitrust claims outright. In essence, this court ruling unofficially looked upon the Tennis Council as the sole governing body of men's pro tennis, with Happer in essence its commissioner, having the ability to represent pro tennis in formulating rules designed to improve the sport and ensure its future. This legal ruling essentially puts agents, players, and potential tournament sponsors on notice that if they do anything that detracts from the professional game of tennis as stated by the MTC, they will be subject to appropriate penalties and sanctions.

This judicial decision is a positive one for the future of pro tennis. Although the sport has been "open" and had professional status for two decades, until now too many remnants of its amateur past have certainly been bogging it down.

Unlike professional baseball, football, and basketball, pro tennis has been comparatively unregulated and lacking in any sort of specific aim or firm direction. This is surprising, considering that it's a $35 million industry. For too many years, the sport has operated with unpaid volunteers and has never had a designated commissioner or any appointed or elected leader with any clout. This is the reason agents have done so well for themselves.

As tennis is becoming more professional, it has signed six full-time umpires, and made sure that linespeople are truly versed in their task by providing schooling and also paying them for their work.

Being professional also means codifying rules of conduct and having the power to enforce these rules just as it's done in professional baseball, football, and basketball. Before the 1987 court ruling against Volvo, the MTC had been virtually powerless to stop IMG and Pro-Serv from doing whatever they wanted. Ironically, the lawsuit brought on by the agents gave the MTC some of the vital strength it needs. It can now protect itself a little better and start enacting some rulings that really have impact, such as its newest one regarding agent activity.

"From now on, you can either represent players or you can put on tournaments. You can't do both," says Marshall Happer. The sooner pro tennis is able to extricate itself from the grasp of the agents, the better off the sport will be. Marshall Happer and the Council agree. Starting in the 1989 calendar year, the MTC's new Conflict of Interest Rule will go into effect. For the first time, agents will be prohibited from involvement in the management or ownership of any tennis tournament. What a great move forward this is!

This ruling represents a critical step in curtailing the power of agents, because it finally gets agents back into the job of strictly representing players and takes them away from their heretofore lucrative position of getting paid for managing tournaments.

After 1989, when anyone applies for a license to put on one of the official Grand Prix tournaments, they will have to provide detailed information for the Council, which will point out exactly who is going to run the tournament. Under the new ruling, anybody but agents can help out in this regard. Says William Babcock, the assistant administrator of the MTC, "This will finally get the gray or cloudy area out of the tournament business by making it free and fair competition. No longer will agents have an extra unfair leverage over a tournament by being able to run a tournament and also arbitrarily offer or withhold players from the tournament as they see fit."

Although the MTC is showing signs of making strides in certain areas, it has yet to have much impact on TV coverage, the game's most vital link to millions of tennis fans. In too many instances, television provides a sometimes biased, self-serving viewpoint in the guise of sports reportage. Although this may seem a small point to some, it must be addressed if tennis wants to be as professional as possible.

For the casual tennis fan, the conflict of interest involving agents who work as TV commentators during matches in which their clients are playing has no detrimental effect—unless, of course, the viewer happens to be one of those who try to figure out which TV analyst has any credibility left. The following example is a good case in point. The Washington Tennis Patrons, a local group in Washington, D.C., has been sanctioned by the MTC to put on the Sovran Bank/D.C. National Tennis Classic in the nation's capital. The Tennis Patrons in turn contracted with ProServ to organize the event for them in 1987. This deal also entitled ProServ to a share in the tournament profits. It wasn't a coincidence that many ProServ players showed up to play.

This was not an unusual arrangement, but it annoyed Marshall Happer. Although IMG and ProServ have offered their managerial services as tournament consultants worldwide for a number of years, it was deals such as this that eventually led to the enactment of the conflict of interest ruling for 1989.

After this particular Sovran tournament had ended, Ivan Lendl, a ProServ client who had beaten Brad Gilbert, also an agency client, was being interviewed by Donald Dell, who just happened to be the TV analyst for the tournament. Dell gushed on air that Lendl had not only played exceptionally well in winning the Sovran tournament, but that even though he had lost at Wimbledon several weeks before, he had been the best player there. Dell's flattery put Lendl in an awkward

position, because the decisive Wimbledon victory of
Australia's Pat Cash over Lendl 7–6, 6–2, 7–5 (Cash lost
a total of 15 points on serve) was still fresh in the mind
of every tennis fan, especially Lendl. Cash had been so
overpowering on Centre Court that day in June that
there was really no doubt about who was the better
player.

Viewers who watched Dell and thought he was an
impartial analyst must have been surprised by this excessive back patting. Didn't Dell know that Cash was
better than Lendl at Wimbledon? Or did he think the
TV audience just wouldn't know better? In any event,
Lendl was quick to thank his agent for the praise, but
had the graciousness to remind Dell that since Cash
had won Wimbledon, it was in fact Cash who was the
best player at Wimbledon in 1987.

13
Televisiontennis

My first television broadcast for CBS was quite an experience. It was 1972, and about 10 TV types were sitting with me around a conference table at the Breakers Hotel in Palm Beach, Florida. I was introduced to the production staff and Pat Summerall, the former New York Giant football kicker who had become one of the network's premier sports commentators. Over the next two days, I would be working on mixed doubles matches featuring the best women in the world teamed up with some 35-and-over men. We would tape for two days, and then it would be edited into a one-hour show for later broadcast.

For an hour, the men talked about how the show would be structured, which cameras, billboards, and modems would be used. I sat there bemused. The longer they talked, the more confusing the TV lingo became; they might as well have been speaking to me in Russian.

I hadn't thought it would be anything like this when I contacted CBS Sports out of the blue several months earlier. The reason I had telephoned was really because of frustration at the way I saw a match being covered one afternoon. Let's say it was Stan Smith versus Rod Laver, where Laver had come to the net on a short approach shot and Smith had quickly zinged one right by him. The announcer had gotten excited and said that it was a great passing shot. I sat there in my living room talking back to the TV set, just as I had many times before when watching tennis. "It was only a routine shot that any good player would be expected to make," I remember saying. "And in this particular case, it wasn't so much a good passing shot, as it was a poor approach by Laver."

A few days later I called a CBS producer in New York with some of my ideas about what could be done to improve television tennis. He appreciated what I had to say about their production and flew me to New York for an interview. A few months later, I was told to report to Florida for my first show. And here we were.

Just before the production meeting broke up, the producer asked if anyone had any questions.

"What was all that you guys were talking about?" I asked. "I really have no idea of what's going on or what I'm supposed to do tomorrow on the broadcast. I hope someone will fill me in."

Everyone laughed at this. Pat Summerall came over and clapped me on the back. "Don't worry, you'll do all right," he said and then walked out of the room.

"Welcome to network television!" I thought to myself as I walked across the street the next day and headed to the courts. I was dressed in my blue CBS Sports blazer and tie. The producer quickly steered me over to a 35-foot-high wooden tower and told me to go right up. I

Pat Summerall and I have worked together since 1972 on televised tennis. Prior to going to the New York Giants football team, Pat played football and also varsity tennis at the University of Arkansas.

was sure none of the Flying Wallendas would ever have attempted this ascent. "Your seat is up there," he said, pointing skyward, and then he showed me the ladder running up the back of the rig.

I cautiously made my way up. After reaching the top, I found to my dismay that there was no railing to grab onto to pull myself up. The ladder just ended. I tugged at a bar at the edge of the platform, threw my right leg over, and just rolled over on my back onto the platform. Certainly not a gracious entrance, but practical.

After I finished brushing the dirt off my jacket and trousers, I gave a quick look around "Broadcast Central." There were two aluminum folding chairs, one camera, two headsets, a table, and what appeared to be miles of cables all over the wooden floor. I sat down, pushed my chair back, and only for the grace of God was I able to keep myself from toppling off the back of the platform and save my budding career. Ten seconds later, with beads of perspiration on my forehead and visions of my lifetime still flickering before me, the red light came on, and I started my first TV broadcast.

Since we were taping the matches, there were no commercials at court changes. Instead, the producer would announce in our headsets, "Hold," "Fill," "Hold," "Cue," and we'd start commentary on the next game. It was confusing for me, and at times I wasn't sure when I could or couldn't talk.

Shortly after the first match started, there was a good rally, and Pat Summerall suddenly looked out of the corner of his eye and saw my head coming down toward his lap. He wasn't sure what was happening, and after the exciting rally had ended, I straightened up again in my seat. This episode was repeated two or three more times, each time on exciting points. Finally, Pat looked at me kind of funny and said that he had heard that some tennis players running around in little white shorts were "suspect." He then took off his headset and jabbed me in the ribs with his elbow for emphasis. Annoyed at his reaction, I did the same to him. "What the hell are you doing, and what do you have in mind?" he said.

Finally realizing what he was talking about, I pointed down to the television cables at Pat's feet. "You're standing on my cable!" I said.

Summerall looked down and soon started to laugh. It seemed that every time there was a good point, Pat stomped his feet in excitement, his big shoes going right on top of my headset cable, which was suspended a few inches off the ground under his chair. Rather than let my head be yanked off my shoulders, I gave way to his foot pressure, with my head almost ending up in his lap each time.

Pat apologized and clapped me on the shoulders, and we've been best of friends ever since.

"Jolly good shot! A brilliant maneuver by Cash!" or something to that effect, said the BBC announcer in his clipped, eloquent tone. The British Broadcasting Corporation has the best televised tennis coverage. The BBC also has the best announcers—at least that's what a lot of people tell me.

I don't believe it for a minute. I'm easily annoyed when I hear how good the BBC is in their coverage and how bad American television is for tennis. Granted, the Brits do a remarkable job with their tennis programming. But what most people tend to overlook is that the BBC is government-owned and therefore doesn't run the commercials that pop up on our shows at every court change. Turn on the set in England, and you get little commentary during play, but at every changeover there is a crisp synopsis about what just transpired.

On CBS we don't have this journalistic privilege. The U.S. Open rights cost CBS many millions a year, so in order to recoup this investment, the company sells air time to advertisers. And so, while the players towel off and rinse their mouths between games, English viewers learn why Boris Becker changed from a topspin to a slice backhand. In America, however, viewers are subjected to a man in a three-piece Brooks Brothers suit telling them why they'd be better off using a particular brokerage firm, a woman talking about deodorant, and someone else telling them how much they really need a $60,000 car.

During my broadcasts, the time in which I can speak is limited. If I'm going to add to the telecast, and that's what I'm hoping to do—add, not just talk—I have to fit my comments and observations between the points, which must be started within 30 seconds, and before we break for commercials. I try not to talk when the ball is in play. The viewers at home have eyes, and they certainly don't need me chattering along with the ball in play. My worth as a commentator is with analysis, at offering insight into what I see unfolding on the court. As I sit in the booth, I'm always looking for trends, changes in a player's strategy, and tactical maneuvers that viewers might be unaware of. I try to point out things that I think will have impact on the match as it unfolds and add to our viewer's enjoyment.

As a former player, I hope I bring something extra to tennis commentary that the typical commentator never can. When Lori McNeil moves up several feet behind the service line on Steffi Graf's second serve, this immediately tells me that McNeil has little respect for the serve, that she's going to chip and charge the net. I know exactly what both women are feeling, in part because I've been in their shoes many times before. McNeil is sending an out and out challenge to Graf, in essence saying, "You're going to have to pass me if you want to beat me." I try to relay these strategies and convey these feelings to the audience. My tone is conversational, not confrontational, and this is pretty much how I earn my keep at CBS.

Preparing for a big tournament is an ongoing, year-round job. In addition to covering the U.S. Open and a couple of other events for CBS, I also do the Italian and French Opens in the springtime, followed by Wimbledon in early summer. I cover five other tournaments throughout the year for Channel 9, Australia's most popular sports network. By the time I tally the number of corporate outings in which I come to give talks and tennis instruction, I end up spending about half the year on the road with tennis.

To keep abreast of what's going on in the tennis world, I'm constantly clipping magazine and newspaper articles that I think are germane and interesting and putting them into a folder I carry with me. When I get to a tournament, I try to talk to as many of the players as I can, as well as their coaches and trainers, in an effort to get a sense of conditioning, game plans, and mental frame of mind.

Once I'm finally settled in the booth and the red light goes on, it's good to know that I'm actually overprepared. This is more than a great feeling, as it eventually pays off during the course of the matches. When the time is appropriate—for example, when the camera focuses on Boris Becker and shows him eyeing John McEnroe with a certain amount of contempt—I'll tell how Becker once said that he had "all the respect in the world for McEnroe as a tennis player, but not as a human being." When Ivan Lendl starts to slow down in the third set—which is actually quite rare, because he prides himself so much on his excellent physical conditioning—I can mention my discussion with his physician the night before when the doctor pointed out that Lendl has been debilitated by the flu and that this could hamper his play.

As with other televised sporting events such as golf, baseball, and football, former athletes have moved into the broadcast booth. I've been impressed by many of these people, but at times I've also found that some working in televisiontennis either don't want to do the homework that's entailed or must not think it's important. One woman, a former player who moved to the TV booth, was amazed at all of the background information I had accumulated about the players and planned to use in my broadcast. She had done nothing to prepare herself and expected just to wing it when the red light went on. When she saw my notes, she wanted to borrow them, which I found to be a bit annoying.

Perhaps, after being in the athletic spotlight for so many years, some players seem to think that all they have to do is sit down in the booth and start talking. It's not quite that easy, as some of them discover, because this can quickly lead to the mortal sin of talking too much without the facts. Sometimes they'll make the worst mistake of all: talking when the ball is in play.

After incompetence and laziness, my biggest gripe with most commentators and sports broadcasters on TV and radio is that few of them give you the score often enough. They're either too involved with the contest and just forget to do it, or else they feel that the listeners or viewers have been around since the broadcast began and already know the score. Other commentators, some popular ones, in fact, just talk too much. They feel it necessary to chatter away constantly. This may be entertaining, but I feel it does a disservice to the game and the viewers. After all, they're interested in the *game!*

I try to make it a point to give the score of the tennis match as often as possible. I don't go so far as one announcer who used to set a little egg timer down next to his microphone. When the sand ran down to the bottom of the hourglass after every three minutes, he'd announce the score and then flip the glass back over, continuing to repeat the score this way throughout the game.

A recent trend in tennis broadcasting is to have as many as three commentators in the booth at the same time, a condition of overkill. It's as if the network is saying, "OK, we've hired everyone; now you guys try to make it work for yourselves."

This isn't as easy as it might sound. I've never claimed to be the ultimate tennis expert or able to cover every point of view. While one of the other announcers might think it his job to be pushy and assertive in his bid to be the lead announcer, working with other people only makes me bend over backward so the others get equal air time. This burden of having to worry about whose turn it is to talk and then say something appropriate really cuts in on my ability to concentrate on the match.

Sports and sportscasters influence the leisure of Americans in a big way, so much so that most major newspapers now run television sports columns in which the writers regularly critique the TV commentators and their work. (Perhaps the six o'clock news should run a short segment in which the broadcaster critiques the column of the local sports columnist.) I have a bone to pick with those scribes who write that I don't take a stand during the game whenever an instant replay is involved. Although I appreciate the technology involved in television, I've never been a proponent of instant replays in tennis, and for good reason. In far too many cases, they still make it impossible for anyone to come up with a pure black-and-white statement that the ball was conclusively in or out.

In the first set of the singles final of the 1987 U.S. Open, Ivan Lendl was in a tie break and at set point with Mats Wilander. The set had already gone 92 minutes, and there was some feeling that if Wilander won the set, he would be in excellent position to keep Lendl from his third consecutive Open trophy. After a protracted rally, Lendl finally sent a shot that landed close to the sideline, and the linesman called the ball out. This quickly set off an angered protest to the umpire from Lendl, who seemed sure that the ball was good.

From my angle in the booth above the court, I really couldn't tell whether the ball was in or out, and looking at the TV monitor and subsequent replay wasn't conclusive either. I therefore said nothing. One television critic later wrote that I was "soft" and that I should have taken a stand one way or another on the one point that perhaps could have been the psychological turning point of the match. In retrospect, that lost point may have been just what Lendl needed. He went on to win the second set convincingly in less than 25 minutes, 6–0. He won the match 6–7, 6–0, 7–6, 6–4.

The comment that I was "soft" annoyed me, however. If I had met that writer in person, I would have told him exactly what I'm writing now: I don't take a stand and never have, unless I firmly believe in what I say.

A similar situation arose years ago in a Davis Cup match while I was serving as team captain. I was sitting courtside right next to the umpire's chair when John McEnroe hit a shot down the opposite sideline and the linesman called it out. McEnroe raced over to the chair and protested that the shot was good, and he then came

While television has brought tennis to the masses and technological innovations such as slow motion and instant replay have added to the viewers enjoyment, it's still often very difficult to tell if a ball is in bounds or out.

to me. and asked me to back him up on the protest. I wasn't able to. I took Mac aside and told him that from where I was sitting there was no way I could tell whether the ball was in or out. I also said that I wasn't going to say it was good just because he was arguing with the chair that it was good. If I was sure it was in, I told McEnroe, I would have argued for him.

I don't view my role as a TV commentator to include airing my opinions about calls anymore than I feel obliged to "say it like it was" in a live match if I didn't see it!

When it comes to televised sports, many viewers and some tennis players think that television alone has the ultimate say regarding which matches are played on which days. This isn't true. With its enormous investment in the U.S. Open, CBS (along with representatives from the two players' associations and the USTA) does retain a strong say about the scheduling of times and the order of matches, but only for a particular day. After all, TV ratings are at stake. For example, suppose a semifinal match involving Swedes ranked number 2 and 3 in the world were scheduled on the stadium court at the U.S. Open for 2:00 P.M. on a Saturday afternoon (prime sports-viewing time), and another semi involved Jimmy Connors, number 6 in the world, going against number 1, Ivan Lendl, at 11:00 A.M. (Saturday morning, kids' cartoon time). You can be sure the network would make every effort to push for a switch in order to get Connors, an American who could possibly help pull in a larger audience, on at prime time and put the Swedes on against the cartoons.

To the annoyance of Mats Wilander, that's exactly what happened at the U.S. Open in 1987. Because of the strong threat of rain, Wilander and Stefan Edberg were told that theirs would be the first match of the day and that it would be moved up an hour to 10:00 A.M., admittedly an unusually early start for a match. This change was the USTA's move, not CBS's, and it was deemed necessary to try to ensure that the other men's semi, Connors-Lendl, would go on early in the afternoon, and also that the women's final could be squeezed in before the predicted rains came.

The 23-year-old Wilander didn't see it quite the same way, however. He was able to convince his fellow countryman, Edberg, who had won a long, hard-fought doubles final the afternoon before, to stay in the locker room with him, and together they staged a miniprotest for having to play so early in the morning. However, after some talk with tournament officials, the Swedes finally took to the court 15 minutes behind schedule, playing their match without further incident. As it turned out, the rains did come later in the afternoon shortly after Navratilova had won her fourth Open trophy and we had gone off the air. With hindsight, rescheduling the matches turned out to be the correct call that day.

I was a little upset with Wilander's actions. Another example of a spoiled pro player showing his displeasure at "drastic" changes in his schedule? I think so. Losing the star billing and going on as a "warm-up" for the main act, instead of being the main act, is disheartening. And granted, 10:00 A.M. is an early start, but with the weather circumstances, it was necessary, and Wilander should have understood that. It was early for Wilander's opponent as well, so he shouldn't have been doing all that griping. None of the pro players are mistreated, and no one should think they are. In some cases, a pro just has to go along with what's best for pro tennis and follow the orders, even if they are unpleasant or inconvenient. That's just part of being a pro in a lucrative game that's been popularized and supported to a large extent by television and a TV audience.

14
Tennis Fitness

Not all players on the pro tour are in great shape. After the top 30 men in the world, the rest are probably not in as good physical condition as they could be.

If you want to be the best in tennis, you have to spend a lot of time off the court with training that will specifically help develop improved on-court performance. This kind of nontennis work includes things like running sprints, skipping rope, doing push-ups and sit-ups, and possibly even beginning a weight-training program to improve overall strength. Many of today's players don't do any of this extra work, and it clearly shows in their ranking.

The tennis season runs year-round. Unlike other elite athletes, tennis players really don't have an off-season during which they can kick back and do absolutely nothing. The Australian Open, the first of the four Grand Slam tournaments, unofficially opens each new

season in mid-January. The French Open follows almost half a year later in May. Wimbledon comes in late
June, and the U.S. Open starts by late August. Scattered
in between are week-long tournaments in different
parts of the world. There's a demanding clay-court circuit in Europe, Davis Cup play in different regions of
the globe, and also a popular indoor series in Europe
and another in North America that take players right
through to the next new season.

A tennis pro who feels burnout coming on as a result
of overpractice and overplay must find the appropriate
time between tournaments to rest, or else just take a
week or two off. If a player needs extra work on a weakness, he or she has to make the time and get it done. By
carefully picking and choosing beforehand which tournaments to enter, a player can judge when to begin an
intensive physical training program to prepare for these
matches.

When I played, we didn't have today's style of trainers
and coaches who can outline what's needed in order to
get in shape. I used to devise my own regime based on
what I had picked up from playing basketball in high
school and college, and from what I had seen or heard
other tennis players were doing.

Running up and down stadium steps was big on my
conditioning program, because I felt that it best built
up my endurance and also made me mentally tough.
Anyone who's raced up several hundred stairs, come
back down slowly, and then sprinted up again and
again with lungs burning and thighs turned to mush is
certainly toughened in body and soul.

I also used to jump rope almost every day, trying to
get in a few hundred skips. This usually took about 10
minutes and really got me sweating. Skipping rope is
great for building stamina as well as for increasing
coordination, and I still recommend it.

Lifting weights has become popular with some players on the tour, but even though I was built like a football player, I admit it didn't come from pumping iron. I
never touched weights, because I was afraid that it
would tighten up my shoulder muscles. When I hear of
players pushing heavy weights, I get nervous because I
think it can detract from the fluid motion that you need
to develop in your swing, especially in your serve. Other
than doing sit-ups or push-ups, I never really did anything special to work on my stomach or arm muscles.

Pro players can go very far with natural ability, but
they'll usually be held back from winning consistently
if they're not in good physical shape. Harry Hopman,
the fabled Australian coach, had many talented players
under his tutelage in a career as Davis Cup captain that
stretched from the late 1930s to the late 1960s. Hop was
a good friend and disciple of Percy Cerutty, the great
Australian track coach, and what made the Australians
some of the toughest players in the world was no doubt
the way Hop worked them extremely hard off the court,
using many of Cerutty's conditioning ideas.

Although Hop may not have been the greatest tennis
strategist, he understood better than anyone how to get
his players ready and peaked to play all of the big
matches. Above all, Hop was a fanatic for fitness. The
foundation for most of his off-court workouts included
dreaded sprints up and down the sand dunes that are so
plentiful and accessible on the Australian coast. As a
result of all this running, many of the Aussies that I
faced ran like deer and lasted all day on the courts,
even when we played in the broiling noonday sun.

Among current players, Stefan Edberg is notable for
maintaining a rigorous training program that keeps
him extremely fit. Edberg shies away from all weight
work, because he feels it will hurt his timing. In place of
pumping iron, he uses gravity and the natural resis-

The pro tennis season runs virtually year round and players have to make time for their off-court fitness drills. Stefan Edberg of Sweden doesn't believe in long distance running, but instead performs drills each week that will emphasize explosiveness and power, two qualities that are central to his game. PHOTO COURTESY OF ADVANTAGE INTERNATIONAL tance of his body to help build and strengthen his muscles. For developing strength in his arms and abdominal muscles, he does push-ups and sit-ups.

Edberg isn't a fan of long-distance running, because he feels that it actually makes him lose his court quickness by acclimating his nervous system to running slowly. "Tennis is an explosive sport, so I'm always working on things to develop my quickness," he says.

Throughout the long professional season, Edberg's off-court training includes 1,000 skips a day with a jump rope; a series of 10 wind sprints of 30–40 yards each; and 30–60 "high jumps," jumping up and touching his knees to his chest. The Aussies call these "kangaroo jumps."

Being as physically fit as possible is important, but Edberg feels that the most effective way for him to see improvement in his game is to work as hard as he can on the tennis court: to get ready for the U.S. Open or any Grand Slam event, prior to the tournament he'll usually practice hard for three to four hours a day for five straight days.

Although there are certainly a lot of men on the tour who could use some extra workouts, it's amazing how many more unfit women are on the tour today. After about number 20 in the world rankings, most seem to need a bit of extra work. This could include jogging to build up endurance, running sprints to develop the quick, explosive power needed to chase down balls, and some closer attention to exactly what kind of food is consumed during the day.

Martina Navratilova, the most dominating player ever in the history of the women's game, first found out about the importance of fitness after losing too many matches she felt she could have won if she had had more endurance. Since then, what she's done to improve herself physically has set off reverberations that are still being felt by women who want to unseat her from the top.

For the Czech star, 1981 wasn't a particularly good year. Without a doubt, Navratilova had an abundance of talent (she had been ranked number 1 in the world two years earlier), but she was now frustrated by her inconsistent play. During a brief changeover in the first set of the finals of the 1981 Canadian Open, Navratilova told her friend Nancy Lieberman, "I'm pooped. I can hardly breathe." Navratilova went on to lose the tournament to Tracy Austin 6–2, 6–3.

"After she told me that she felt winded, it hit me like a lightning bolt," recalled Lieberman. "It had never occurred to me that a world-class tennis player could ever be physically out of shape." Lieberman, a Far Rockaway, New York basketball whiz considered by many the best American player ever to have played women's basketball, agreed to go to work with Navratilova immediately to help build up her stamina.

Tennis is an individual sport, and many players, being less self-motivated than other athletes, push themselves only as hard as they want to. Lieberman's background was basketball, which has a totally different mind-set. Teammates and competitors are going hard all of the time, and players who don't keep up with the pace get dropped very quickly.

The physical transformation of Navratilova took from 1981 to 1984. Along the way, a lot of grunting and groaning went on within the confines of the gym. Workouts were grueling, consisting of a lot of sprinting on a track at all distances up to 600 yards. Navratilova lifted weights for upper-body strength and did barbell lunges to develop stronger legs.

Navratilova also radically changed her diet with the

help of Robert Haas, a writer specializing in nutrition, and later with Aspen, Colorado, internist, Harold C. Whitcomb, Jr., M.D., a physician who specializes in chemical imbalances in the body. Favorite Czech dishes packed with calories and fats were eliminated in favor of pasta, whole grains, and skim-milk cheeses, while she cut back her intake of red meat and refined sugars.

For such a great athlete, Navratilova's footwork in tennis used to be relatively poor. What saved her was her tremendous stroke production and natural ability. Basketball therefore became a key element in Navratilova's off-court training. By playing defense against Lieberman in countless one-on-one basketball games, Navratilova apparently learned proper foot movement, how to shuffle her feet from side to side to get into proper position. She soon started to move her feet the same way on the tennis court.

Navratilova's off-court training paid handsome dividends. For a five-year stretch from 1982 to 1986, she was ranked number 1 in the world. She won Wimbledon a record six straight times, including her 1987 7–5, 6–3 triumph over newest rival, 18-year-old Steffi Graf. She also won the U.S. Open Singles crown in 1983–1984 and followed up again in 1986 and 1987.

Navratilova was certainly a revolutionary in women's tennis fitness. She broke new ground, which then gave direction to all the other top women and helped them push to new physical levels as well in order to keep up with her.

By 1985 Hana Mandlikova of Czechoslovakia clearly understood exactly what physical fitness had done for Navratilova's tennis. "I used to work out before," she said shortly before the 1987 U.S. Open, "but never as much as I do now." Beginning in early 1985, Mandlikova started concentrated off-court physical work, which she credits with helping her win her first U.S. Open Singles title that same year. Currently one of the top players in the world, she still has her best tennis ahead of her.

From what I've observed in Mandlikova's career to date, I'd say that off-court exercise has definitely made her a quicker player and helped her develop more endurance than she's ever exhibited. Now when she plays two tough matches back to back, she doesn't appear to be tired or stiff. Knowing that you're not going to be fatigued on the court is a great boost for a player—it becomes possible to concentrate totally on tennis.

Mandlikova was sidelined most of the 1987 spring and early summer season with a nagging foot injury that flared up in May and later forced her to drop out of the French Open, the first Grand Slam she won in 1981, and miss Wimbledon. Once the foot healed, however, she returned to Holland with coach Betty Stove to begin a daily three-hour conditioning program along with some Dutch soccer players.

Each workout started with 45 minutes of stretching to music to get the muscles warm and the body limber. Later, trotting down to a nearby beach, she ran wind sprints in the sand until her tongue was hanging out. When that was finished, she went back to the gym to lift weights and do plyometric drills, a series of jumping exercises that strengthen the legs and help develop the quick starts needed in tennis.

These off-court drills were rigorous, but they were just what Mandlikova needed to get back in tournament-playing condition. Once on the tour, she cut back on the intensity of her off-court workouts and concentrated on her tennis practice, a routine that sometimes lasts four hours a day. In addition to keeping in shape by playing this much tennis, she still relies on simple fitness drills that she can do on the court.

After tennis practice ends each day, Mandlikova starts her drills by running from the baseline to the net, from the service line to the net, and then from one side of the court to the other. Holding her racket and taking slashing forehand and powerful backhand swings, she duplicates at high running speeds the winning moves she plans to use in upcoming matches. There are no crowds to cheer her on, and it often hurts to continue. But she knows that this is what she has to do to get to the top, so she does it willingly.

As soon as players lose this desire to put in the extra work, they're in trouble. With so many hungry players in the game today, a player who lets up even a little is liable to be leapfrogged by another player more eager for success.

When it comes to fitness for recreational tennis, you have to honestly ask yourself: how fit do I really want to be? Do I want to be able to play three sets of hard singles on a summer afternoon and not feel like I've been run over by a truck when it's all finished? Or are my aims a little lower? You may want to be able to go for two sets of fast-paced doubles every other day and not be winded from the experience.

In either case, you'll have to do something to build up your aerobic, or cardiovascular, capabilities. This means that you will have to run, ride a bike, swim, or take an aerobics class in order to increase the ability of your lungs and heart to supply blood to your exercising muscles. The more you do this, the stronger your heart and lungs will become, and consequently the less fatigued you will eventually be on the tennis court.

Unlike a running or jogging program, a regular swimming program offers tremendous aerobic benefits without unduly stressing the body. This makes it an excellent exercise for overweight people, as well as people who are injured or suffering from arthritis. Many nonswimmers tend to dismiss swimming, especially lap swimming, as boring. To the contrary, swimming offers a feeling of weightlessness, of floating in inner space, a sensation that's unattainable from any other exercise. Swimmers who put in workouts several times a week year-round do so in a pleasant, semitrance state, almost hypnotized by the regular rhythm of armstrokes, kicks, and breathing.

If you can't swim regularly, then try walking briskly, jogging, bicycling, or taking part in an aerobics class three times a week, working out at 75 percent of your maximum heart rate for at least 20–30 minutes a session. According to the latest medical findings, you will be doing the minimum amount of exercise necessary for good health. This exercise will also help you get through your doubles match without feeling as if you've just run a marathon.

If you're looking to play a more competitive game of tennis, you'll have to increase your physical training and up the amount of time you put in on the court in practice. A problem to avoid in this case is trying to do too much too soon.

Has this ever happened to you? You go to the court for the first time after a long layoff, and for an hour or so, you hit hard and chase down balls that a few months ago were no problem to reach. And although you feel fine on the court, you spend the next few days with sore muscles, as you pay off a debt for having tried to recapture the glory days of your past without having properly prepared your body.

I'm always telling players to approach tennis gradually if they've been inactive. Holding back on your enthusiasm the first few times out on the court helps you avoid the overall stiffness that seems to come during early-season play.

Don't play tennis to get in shape. Get in shape to play tennis. Of course, one of the best ways to be in shape for tennis is never to get out of shape in the first place. A growing number of tennis players are finding out that this is best accomplished by toning up and keeping fit at home. No longer dependent on good weather and shunning the glitz, glamor, and long lines and appointments that often come with traditional health club memberships, these players are opting instead to work out at home on their own time on scaled-down versions of exercise equipment found in the best clubs.

Although they can certainly get fit doing push-ups and chin-ups and skipping rope, some people are bypassing this "no-tech" route to good health and going high-tech by outfitting their homes with computerized rowers, stationary bicycles, motorized treadmills, cross-country ski machines, and gleaming chrome weight machines. Some people go further with their home gyms by knocking down walls, raising ceilings, adding wall-to-wall carpeting, saunas, and Jacuzzis. They often justify the expense by saying that the gym will motivate them to keep their New Year's resolutions to exercise and improve their tennis game.

Unfortunately, it takes more than thousands of dollars worth of exercise equipment to make an exercise program last. Exercise is work, and too many people think that the machines will do it for them. The disappointing reality is perhaps the main reason a good number of rowing machines eventually end up supporting flower pots instead of sweating bodies.

15
Tennis Anyone?

Here's my key to success for all weekend players: try like crazy on the court, but most of all make sure that you're having fun. This is all that you can really ask from tennis. Unfortunately, it's a hard idea to instill in many people.

Since my retirement as a pro player, I've kept active by playing tennis and some golf, but strictly for fun and enjoyment. My competitive side, I must admit, has all but dried up. Playing tennis used to be a way of life and a livelihood. But I was forever pushed, by myself and by my competitors. Now when I play, I no longer want to be under pressure. I view tennis simply as a vehicle that gets me out, gives me some valuable exercise, and allows me to be around people I like.

Weekend players should keep their tennis playing in perspective. The main reasons you're out there are physical and social. When you're on the courts, it shouldn't be World War III as it is on the pro tour. Of course, you should try to do your best and try to win. But don't make the all-too-common mistake of thinking you've had a good time only if you win.

Realistically, few people put in enough time with practice, and not many are overly skilled at tennis to begin with. Therefore it's a mistake to base the success of a day on winning a tennis match. Do your best, but don't go home and kick the dog or yell at your spouse and kids because you lost a match. It just doesn't make sense.

There's no reason to be miserable after a match. Seldom do people ever play up to what they think their potential is, because most people have such an inflated idea of their potential that they'll never achieve it. The result is perpetual frustration.

Often at clinics, recreational players will ask me how to make the best use of their weekly court time they have. My first response is to tell them to try to play at least three times a week, on Saturday and Sunday, and again on Wednesday if possible. By keeping this kind of schedule, you'll never be away from the game for more than two days at a time and will be able to develop some sort of continuity. You'll also have more time to work on personal game weaknesses, to discover your strengths, and to chart your progress.

Another way to make the most of your time is to be ready to start playing as soon as you take to the court. Don't waste valuable court time that you're paying for—or may have had to wait over an hour for—while you go through preparatory muscle-stretching drills.

I'm noticeably slower than I used to be on the court. Over the years, I've added a few pounds and lost a few steps with a surgically repaired knee. However, when I come to play, I make up for this with one of my major weapons: physical preparation. When I step on the

Go to the court already warmed up and ready to begin play. Five to 15 minutes of light jogging, rope skipping, stretching, and calisthenics will get you properly loosened up before you start swinging at the ball. I've been doing it for years. PHOTO COURTESY OF THE TRABERT ARCHIVES.

court, I'm already loosened up and ready to play in a relatively short period of time.

Many players complain that they go through an unsatisfactory first set because they feel stiff or sluggish, but by the second set, when they're finally ready to go at it, their court time runs out and they have to leave. The result is an unsatisfactory workout. To combat this problem, stretch and jog in place before playing. This will help loosen up your body and build up a light sweat. That way, once you're on the court you hit a few balls and then you're ready to go.

When traveling on the Kramer tour, I carried my jump rope with me and skipped just before I had to go out on the court. This would loosen most of the kinks I'd developed from hours of driving. Skipping also raised my heart rate and got me in a competitive frame of mind.

Never go on the court "cold." If your body hasn't been properly prepared for all the twisting, turning, jumping, sliding, and running you expect to do during the next few sets, you can't perform at your best.

Think of a fine-tuned car sitting out all night on the street with the temperature at a frigid 15 degrees. The oil in the motor block is cold and sluggish. Just because you put the key in the ignition, you can't expect the car to turn right over and accelerate from 0 to 60 in six seconds. You have to let it idle for a while, stepping on the accelerator every now and then to let the motor heat up. After some time, you're finally able to put it in gear and pull out. You've warmed it up properly.

Your body is like this car. The lubricating fluid in the joints has to be warmed first. The muscles have to be gently moved, stretched, and loosened before you start jamming on the accelerator and racing around the tennis court.

A 5- to 10-minute routine I do before I play has

worked wonders for me. I spend half of my warm-up time slowly jogging in place. Then I'll swing my racket several times back and forth with the cover still on to increase the wind resistance. This mimics my swing motion and gets my shoulders and elbow warm and loose. Some doctors believe that this simple exercise is a great way to strengthen the forearm and wrist, which might help protect you from tennis injury.

Based on my experience and observation, failure to properly warm up before beginning to hit hard could be a major cause of tennis elbow, the scourge of the weekend player. According to a medical study I read, tennis elbow hits 45 percent of nontournament players who play tennis daily. This ailment is thought to be brought on by excessive strain of the muscles attached to the outer part of the elbow. This strain can be brought on by a mishit, poor technique, the impact of a ball traveling at 50–60 miles per hour into your weak backhand shot, or the impact of your racket on the ball at service.

Besides limbering up, another precaution is to make sure that your tennis balls are fairly new. Once the balls become wet or lose pressure, switch to new ones. Playing with a heavy ball will only strain your arm, a condition that could ultimately bring on tennis elbow.

In addition, check the tension on your strings. Generally, the higher the string tension, the more strain you will put on your arm because of the vibration from the racket at impact with the ball. To overcome this, you might keep the tension down to about 52 to 55 pounds for normal-sized rackets, a little higher for midsized or oversized rackets. Looser string tension reduces vibration, which will mean less strain and pain for your arm.

Except for one case of bursitis in my shoulder, I've never had major medical problems brought on by tennis. When you look at the available statistics covering injuries to tennis players, I guess I can count myself lucky. Of course, the warm-ups supplement the luck.

When I start to hit on the court with my opponent, I begin gently. Once I finally feel comfortable, my arm feels good, and my legs are loose, I'll gradually increase the pace of my returns. Pretty soon, I'm ready to play a set.

Recreational tennis can provide a demanding aerobic, or cardiovascular, workout if you remember to keep one thing in mind: keep moving at all times on the court. Run as hard as you can to get behind balls hit to you. In addition to beneficially taxing your heart, lungs, and other vital organs, getting behind the ball as much as possible will increase the power of your shot.

Running also will help your volleying. Run in and pick the ball off before it bounces, and you'll add a new, possibly dangerous shot to your game. When you come in and get lobbed over, don't just stand there watching the ball sail over your head and hoping it will land out of bounds. Run the ball down! Some balls just might stay in bounds, and you'll have a chance to salvage a few points if you're willing to put out some extra effort.

Finally, after a point is scored, jog to the net to pick up any errant balls. Tennis players waste too much time walking, oh, so casually to get stray balls. During their strolls, they're often easily distracted and start to chat with a friend on an adjacent court. While this may say something about the social aspect of tennis, it says little about providing a good workout. However, if you remember to run as much as you can on the court—whether to go after balls in play or out—you'll be doing a lot to ensure your own physical fitness.

A problem more common among weekend players than the pros is the inability to adapt readily to different playing surfaces. When I was playing, we had to play on all types of surfaces. There were few clay- or grass-court specialists, because being amateurs and trying to improve daily, the top players played in all of the tournaments, no matter what the surface. It usually took me several minutes to feel comfortable with a new surface, but after that I paid it no heed. Today's successful pro is equally adaptable.

Weekend players seldom have a choice when it comes to playing surface, and they often bounce from indoors to outdoors, from Har Tru to Deco Turf, concrete to clay. Weekend players who play clay often have a difficult time switching to concrete. The ball comes bouncing up quickly and before the player can even get his or her racket back, the ball has gone by for a point.

Don't feel bad if this happens to you. That's why you're a club player and not out on the tour. Only with time and experience will you learn how to play all the surfaces.

A good tip for moving between the different surfaces: if you have limited time to warm up on the new court, don't spend much of it volleying at the net. Instead, move back to the baseline and hit from there. Watch especially how the ball hits the ground and what it does when it bounces up toward you. Doing this for at least five minutes will give you an opportunity to see how it differs from what you're used to and to adjust accordingly. Early racket preparation is the key to success here. Don't forget to keep your eyes on the ball as well.

As a rule, when you play on clay—a surface that's almost becoming an endangered species in this country—you need plenty of patience. When your opponent hits the ball to you, prepare your body and racket early, then hold, hold, hold until the ball finally comes up and you're ready to swing at it. The ball will bounce higher on clay—often up near your shoulders—and when you go to hit it, you've got to be patient. Because of the higher bounce and less pace, it's harder to hit back winners than it is on a faster surface.

On the other hand, if you go from clay to cement or grass, the ball will move much faster and lower, and you have to be ready for it much sooner. Get set up for the ball quickly. The ball's bounce will be quicker and lower on cement and grass, so you must have your racket back as early as you can. Naturally, you'll have to start your forward swing sooner.

Careful off-court preparation has kept me injury-free and helped me sustain my enjoyment of tennis all these years. I'm surprised, therefore, to see people rush onto the court at their appointed hour, lazily hit a few balls, and then start trying to play full tilt. Not only is an aging body unprepared for this crazy demand, but it might rebel by having the Achilles tendon snap. Or at the least, these players wind up with shoulder, leg, or back muscles inflamed to the point of temporary incapacitation.

Give yourself a little extra time and arrive earlier than usual for your match. Warm up and get a good sweat going before you go on the court. You'll find that your game will improve and you'll have more fun playing. Wear a sweater or sweatsuit to speed up your warm-up, and put it back on when you cool down, so that your muscles will stay warm and supple.

Another big mistake weekend players make is to try to emulate a pro player they have seen playing on television. Consistency in stroke production should be your main concern, not whether you can hit a topspin lob like Ivan Lendl.

Whenever I give a clinic, people ask me how they can perfect this topspin lob. I just tell them to put it out of their minds. The percentage of lobs ever made successfully with excessive topspin is extremely low. Granted, the ones that the pros do make are sensational, and people talk about them and remember them. However, people should also remember the majority of topspin lobs that come up short or go flying way out of bounds.

If you're a weekend player and really want to improve your game, I strongly recommend that you work on your backhand. This is usually a weekend player's weak link and the main reason for losing so many games. Surprisingly, on the pro level, the backhand is usually the stronger groundstroke because it's the easiest shot to reproduce so consistently.

Here's why a backhand is easier to hit than a forehand: the backhand is mechanically an easier shot because you take the racket back, keeping your free hand on the throat of the racket so you can actually feel where the racket is. The right arm (for a right-handed player) stays close to the body, another important control mechanism. Once you start to swing, no part of the body is ever in the way, as it is with the forehand. Contacting the ball a foot or so in front of you enables you to see the ball better.

I've never been a big fan of the two-handed backhand for two basic reasons. First, you can't reach as far for a ball when you use two hands, and therefore you have to run much more and be quicker in order to get into position. Second, you generally can't handle the low ball or the wide ball, and you have to let go of the racket with your top hand and end up trying to make a one-handed shot anyway.

The only advantage I can see in a two-fisted backhand is that you can change the direction of the racket head at the last second. But this happens so seldom in the course of a typical match that it's not a good enough reason to teach the stroke. With little children just starting out, I let them hold on with their second hand in order to give a little push, but I always tell them to let go of the racket on the follow-through. As they get older and stronger, I teach only the one-handed backhand.

When it comes to hitting the ball very well with two hands, there have been some prominent exceptions to the rule. When I played, Pancho Segura hit a two-handed forehand and a one-handed backhand. Jack Kramer considered Segura's forehand to be the best individual shot ever developed in tennis, because he'd hit it hard, could place the ball where he wanted, and up until the point of impact, could effectively disguise which way he was going to hit.

While Segura's double-fisted shot helped his game immensely, he didn't develop it expressly to help with placement, but did so out of necessity. Born into a poor family in Ecuador, he later developed rickets as a child. His dad was a caretaker at a local tennis club, and as a youngster Segura started playing with a man's racket he received as a gift. The racket was much too heavy for him to wield with one hand in normal fashion, so Segura held it with two hands on his forehand. Even later, when he grew to be much stronger, Segura continued with his two-handed forehand because it became so successful.

Bjorn Borg went to two hands on his backhand, I'm told, because that's how he held his hockey stick as a youngster playing ice hockey in his native Sweden. Chris Evert developed her two-handed backhand because that's the way she could handle the racket when she started playing on clay at six years of age.

Again, these are only a few exceptions to my feelings about the two-handed backhand. If you are willing to put in the time and work, you might as well do it with the one-handed backhand. It's difficult for many to learn, but you won't go wrong with it once you learn the

proper mechanics and are able to build up some forearm strength. The proper backhand grip is essential.

Proper mechanics in all of your strokes is the key to
consistency for weekend players as well as the pros.
This means not being too "wristy." Sure, bringing your
wrist into play will enable you to hit some sensational
shots if you're lucky, but you'll also hit a much higher
percentage of bad ones.

"But Rod Laver always uses a lot of wrist when he
hits," you might say. Yes, but Laver also has hit eight
jillion tennis balls in his career, practicing as much as
five hours a day. A player who puts in only two hours on
a weekend can never expect to duplicate the shots of a
top pro like Laver. As soon as the weekend player uses
the wrist, he or she rolls the racket over or goes under
the ball and, as a result, makes an error.

It's the dinker who wins all the trophies. Why? Simply
because this player keeps the ball in play the longest,
plays within his or her limitations, and avoids the fancy
shots. Therefore, to develop any kind of consistent play,
your best approach is to play it safe the way the dinker
does. Don't try to hit winners all of the time. Instead of
aiming for three inches from the baseline, try going for
three feet from it. If you have to race after a tough shot,
just try to get the ball back into play instead of trying
for a spectacular shot that you vainly hope will get you
the point. For weekend players, chances are that if you
can just hit the ball back six or seven times, you'll win
the point.

Even though you may have bad knees that beg you to
stop playing, or simply a slightly aging body that goes
putt, putt, putt on the court and prevents you (in your
mind's eye, that is) from duplicating what you see the
pros doing, you can at least try to approximate what the
pros do by preparing yourself mentally every time you

go to play. A good portion of the success that top athletes achieve comes from being relaxed. If you were to analyze your own game, you'd no doubt find that you play some of your best tennis in practice when you're just playing for fun with a friend. This is because you're totally relaxed and haven't put yourself under the mental strain of concern with winning.

Therefore, your mental preparation will play a tremendous role in the eventual outcome of your tennis match. If you can bring the relaxed attitude that you have in practice along with you when you have to play in the big match in a local tournament, your play will be much better. Too often, players who aren't tournament-toughened build up negative scenarios in their minds about how they think they'll play. When they get in the match and find themselves falling behind, they tell themselves, "See, it's just like I said it was going to be," and they talk themselves into losing. This self-fulfilling prophecy needlessly stunts their progress, reduces their enjoyment, and often leads to their downfall.

When you find yourself losing a match, the first thing you should do is take a deep breath, relax, and ask yourself as calmly as you can, "Why am I losing?" Is the other person playing better tennis than you are? Or are you losing because you're not staying within your game plan? If you're a steady player and suddenly start trying for out and out winners, then you're bringing on your own problems. You're disrupting your normal style of play by attempting to do things you ordinarily don't do even in practice.

On the other hand, if you're playing your game fairly well as far as you can tell, but the other person is just playing better, then you need to change your game plan. Don't hesitate; you have nothing to lose. If you're playing a fairly consistent baseline game, for example, then switch and try rushing the net a bit to change the pace a little. Start to increase the pace on your shots. Your main objective should be to mix it up, to keep your opponent guessing by trying something new. After all, whatever you were doing before wasn't working, so using a new strategy may improve your chances.

Recognize also that your game plan may not be working simply because your opponent is outhustling you. In the ensuing games, consciously try to anticipate your opponent's returns and be ready to move quickly.

During a rest period, block out the fact that you're losing and spend the time trying to analyze what you can do to try to start scoring. If you serve and volley and find that when you come in, you're getting passed, ask yourself whether you're getting passed off good serves of your own or whether your serves are landing too short. Is your approach shot deep enough with a little pace on it? Or have you made a short approach shot, which then enables your opponent to pass you?

If your approach shot is good and nothing is wrong with your game plan, you may be losing because you are not executing as well that day. Or you may have been overmatched with an opponent who belongs at the top of the tennis ladder. When this happens, you can't do much except continue to try as hard as you can and try to avoid becoming too discouraged. To boost your morale at times like this, you can say, "I tried everything that I could think of, but today I'm just not good enough."

There's nothing wrong with admitting that to yourself. When you shake hands after the match—although he or she was too good for you this day—you can think "I'll try to get you another time."

Someone has to lose in tennis, but you should never go off the court questioning yourself: why didn't I try a different approach shot? Why did I serve so wide? Why did I float so many balls? Why didn't I go to the net more often? Why didn't I draw him to the net more? Questions that come up after the fact show that you weren't thinking as well as you could have been on the court. In the process of losing, you might as well get some answers to your questions by trying everything that you can to see what exactly will work for you. It's only an exercise in frustration to ask yourself these questions after the match is over.

Sports competition is an inexact science. Often a talented player will lose to a much less gifted opponent simply because the less talented player hustled throughout the match, refusing to give up. When you're on the court, it's not so difficult to try your hardest. You have nothing else to do when you're out there, so you might as well give it your all by running after all the balls and playing as hard as you can. You have all night, maybe even all the next week to rest up, so if you're in good shape, why not go all out, at least for the sake of your pride?

Pride is a big word in sports, just as it is in life. If you have pride in your performance, then even in defeat you can ask no more of yourself. You gave your all in the struggle to win. While I haven't won all of my matches, I have always played the best I could. During one stretch on the pro tour when I lost many times to Pancho Gonzales, I still did everything within my power to win each time that I faced him. Pancho was later quoted in the newspaper as saying that he knew I was going to give him a tough fight in every match and that he always had to be ready for me. This, then, is the essence of sport and competition: both players pushing each other to bring out their highest levels of skill. Give a 100 percent effort when you go out to play. Then you can hold your head up no matter what the final outcome.

Tennis should help relieve stress, not add stress to your life. Therefore, in every tennis tournament that you play, view the matches as competitive, but mainly as a fun way to get some exercise. While these matches may bring on butterflies, don't let them ruin your everyday life.

If you have the right attitude—and this means first and foremost trying to enjoy yourself while playing tennis—you'll be more relaxed and able to perform to the best of your abilities. Win or lose, you'll also find yourself better able to concentrate and less susceptible to distractions and disappointments such as a noisy cheering section or a flubbed overhead. The more you're able to keep this healthy perspective, the more satisfaction you'll get from this great game.

The ball is now in your court. Make the most of it! Have fun!